St.Ignace Parish of Willow Bunch, Saskatchewan

1882-1910

Baptisms, Marriages and Burials

Gail Morin

© 1998

Revised 2016

Source: Family History Center Microfilm #1290091

__, Alexander - B-9, Alexandre __, born 3 March 1886, baptized 24 March 1886, Parents Indian, Godfather: P. St.Germain o.m.i., Godmother: Marie Tanner, Pierre St.Germain o.m.i. (page 10)

__, Anonyme: Infant of Madeleine Bourassa, [no date, but following Leandre Rainville], Pierre St.Germain priest. (page 137)

__, Joseph Thomas Damien Francois: B-21, Joseph Thomas Damien Francois born 21 December 1907, baptized 21 December 1907. (page 53)

__, Antoine "Peid Noir": Antoine "Peid Noir", age 10, buried 1 February 1886, Witness: Antoine Charbonneau, Pierre St.Germain priest. (page 137)

ADAM, Adeline: Adeline Adam, age 21, died 22 May 1905, buried 24 May 1905, Witness: Prudent Lapointe, C. J. Passaplan priest. (page 139)

ADAM, Andre: B-10, Andre Adam (illegitimate), born 22 February 1896, baptized 16 June 1896, son of Moise Adam and an Indian, Godfather: Francois Beaudry, Godmother: Elisa Boyer, Pierre St.Germain o.m.i. (page 28)

ADAM, Louis: B-4, Louis Adam, born 8 December 1885, baptized 16 February 1886, son of Jeremie Adam and Julie Larocque, Godfather: Louis Piche, Godmother: Cecile Desmarais, Pierre St.Germain o.m.i. (page 10)

ADAM, Marie Josephine: Marie Josephine Adam, age 4, buried, 9 October 1895, A. Lerche priest. (page 138)

ADAM, Moise and Isabelle POITRAS: M-4, Moise Adam, son of Baptiste Adam and Marie Bouille (Lac Pelletier), married 6 August 1909, Isabelle Poitras, daughter of Gabriel Poitras and Isabelle Malaterre, Witness: Alfred Lalonde and Albert Rainville, Alphonse Lemieux priest. (page 116)

ADAM, Vitaline: Vitaline Adam, age 2, buried 11 October 1895, A. Lerch priest. (page 138)

ALLARD, Alfred: B-10, Alfred Allard, born 8 June 1891, baptized 10 June 1891, son of Jean Baptiste Allard and Rosalie Fagnan, Godfather: Napoleon Fagnan, Godmother: Guillelmine Fagnan, Pierre St.Germain o.m.i. (page 19)

ALLARD, Louis Napoleon: B-8, Louis Napoleon Allard, born 5 July 1889, baptized 27 July 1889, son of Jean Baptiste Allard and Rosalie Fagnan, Godfather: Napoleon McGillis, Godmother: Philomene McGillis, Pierre St.Germain o.m.i. (page 16)

ALLARD, Magdeleine: Magdeleine Allard, age 2, buried 17 April 1897, Witness: Jean Baptiste Roy, Pierre St.Germain priest. (page 138)

ALLARD, Napoleon: Napoleon Allard, age 3 months, died 8 May 1892, buried 14 May 1892, Witnesses: Jean Baptiste Roy, Pierre St.Germain priest. (page 138)

ALLARD, Theodore: Theodore Allard, age 1, buried 11 October 1895, Witness: Louis Allard, A. Lerch priest. (page 138)

AMYOT, Arthur and Betsy ANDERSON: M-3, Arthur Amyot married 2 March 1883 Elisabeth Anderson (non-Catholic), Pierre St.Germain o.m.i. (page 110)

AMYOT, Francois: B-25, Francois Amyot, born 7 April 1883, baptized 12 September 1883, son of Francois Amyot and Celina Beriault, Godfather: Isidore Amyot, Godmother: Emerise Lavallie, Pierre St.Germain o.m.i. (page 4)

AMYOTTE, Isidore and Octavie CARDINAL: M-3, Isidore Amyotte, son of Joseph Amyotte and Madeleine Hamelin, married 11 February 1884, Octavie Cardinal, daughter of Charles Cardinal and Josette Desmarais, Witness: Joseph Lapointe and Thadse Ouellette, Pierre St.Germain o.m.i. (page 110)

AMYOTTE, Marie and Louis HOULE: M-6, Louis Houle, son of Louis Houle and Marguerite Ross, married 2 September 1883, Marie Amyotte, son of Louis Amyotte and Celina Grandbois [Beriault], Witness: Joseph Short and Zacharie Poitras, Pierre St.Germain o.m.i. (page 110)

AMYOT, Napoleon Paul: B-1, Napoleon Amyot, born 14 January 1884, baptized 15 January 1884, son of Arthur Amyot and Betsy Anderson, Godfather: Joseph Amyot, Godmother: Madeleine Hamelin, Pierre St.Germain. (page 6)

ANDERSON, Betsy and Arthur AMYOT: M-3, Arthur Amyot married 2 March 1883 Elisabeth Anderson (non-Catholic), Pierre St.Germain o.m.i. (page 110)

ANDERSON, Joseph Thomas: B-12, Joseph Thomas Anderson, age 13 years, baptized 10 May 1903, son of Thomas Anderson and Flore Anna Hope, Godfather: Louis Dumais, Godmother: Elisa Caplette, Emmanuel Garon priest. (page 43)

ARCAND, Marie Bernadette and Joseph KRUPPA: M-4, Joseph Kruppa, son of Frank Kruppa and Juliana KJowaczs, married 3 November 1893, Marie Bernadette Arcand, son of Alphee Arcand and Marie Anna Caroline Borne, Witness: Noel Paquin and Amada Paquin, Pierre St.Germain o.m.i. (page 112)

AUGER, Marie Honorine Christine and Leon Alexis GEORGES: M-4, Leon Alexis Georges, son of Alexis Georges and Jeanne Marie Letriquet, married Marie Honorine Christine Auger, daughter of Constantin Auger and Marie Felice _, Witness: Treffle Bonneau, D. A. Godin, Alphonse Lemieux priest. (page 116)

BALAUX, Germaine Marie Louise: B-9, Germaine Marie Louise Balaux, born 2 May 1909, baptized 16 May 1909, daughter of Joseph Balaux and Louise Martin, Godfather: Treffle Bonneau, Godmother: Marie Louise Vaudry, Alphonse Lemieux priest. (page 57)

BALAUC, Louis Joseph Ernest: B-8, Louis Joseph Ernest Balaux, born 23 February 1908, baptized 8 March 1908, son of Joseph Balaux and Louise Martin, Godfather: Louis Balaux, Godmother: Eval Balaux, Alphonse Lemieux priest. (page 54)

BAUDRY, Alfred: B-11, Alfred Baudry, born 12 September 1901, baptized 19 September 1901, son of Noel Baudry and Marie Philomene McGillis, Godfather: Jean Marie Baudry, Godmother: Marie Simpson, Pierre St.Germain o.m.i., married 24 December 1926, Virginie Delorme. (page 39)

BAUDRY, Daniel: B-8, Daniel Baudry, born 13 April 1893, baptized 13 April 1893, son of Noel Baudry and Marie McGillis, Godfather: Napoleon Lafournais, Godmother: Therese McGillis, St.Germain o.m.i. (page 22)

BAUDRY, Joseph: B-19, Joseph Baudry, born 5 September 1902, baptized 13 September 1902, son of Noel Baudry and Philomene McGillis, Godfather: Louis Dumais, Godmother: Louisa _, C. J. Passaplan priest. (page 41)

BAUDRY, Marie Philomene: B-6, Marie Philomene Baudry, born 29 March 1896, baptized 31 March 1896, daughter of Noel Baudry and Marie Philomene McGillis, Godfather: Pierre Tobie McGillis, Godmother: Isabelle

St.Ignace Parish of Willow Bunch, Saskatchewan
1882-1910, Baptisms, Marriages and Burials

Fagnan, A. Leuret priest. (page 28)

BAUDRY, Marie Virginie: B-11, Marie Virginie Baudry, born 29 May 1904, baptized 26 June 1904, Noel Baudry and Marie Philomene McGillis, Godfather: Joseph McGillis, Godmother: Marie McGillis, C. J. Passaplan priest. (page 45)

BAUDRY, Noel and Marie MCGILLIS: M-2, Noel Baudry, son of Baptiste Baudry and Nancy Leveille, married 27 April 1892, Marie McGillis, daughter of Angus McGillis and Isabelle Fagnan, Witness: Napoleon Fagnan and Alexandre Fagnan, Pierre St.Germain o.m.i. (page 112)

BEAUCHAMP, Agnes: Agnes Beauchamp, buried 26 May1901, Witness: Bernard Beauchamp, Pierre St.Germain priest. (page 139)

BEAUCHAMP, Bernard: Bernard Beauchamp, age 35, died 3 April 1902, buried 6 April 1902, Witness: Narcisse Lacerte, Pierre St.Germain priest. (page 139)

BEAUCHAMP, Celina: Celina Beauchamp, age 4, died 27 August 1886, buried 28 August 1886, Witness: Andre Gaudry, Pierre St.Germain priest. (page 137)

BEAUCHAMP, Joseph: B-4, Joseph Beauchamp, born 2 March 1884, baptized 4 March 1884, son of Abraham Beauchamp and Marie Desjardins, Godfather: Athanase Hupee, Godmother: Josette Beauchamp, Pierre St.Germain o.m.i. (page 6)

BEAUCHAMP, Joseph: Joseph Beauchamp, age 7, died 9 February 1892, buried 10 February 1892, Witness: Pierre Bruyere, Pierre St.Germain priest. (page 138)

BEAUCHAMP, Joseph Edmond: B-5, Joseph Edmond Beauchamp, born 12 June 1898, baptized 30 October 1898, son of Bernard Beauchamp and Emma Lacerte, Godfather: Clement Lacerte, Godmother: Eleonore Ouellette, Emmanuel Garon priest. (page 32)

BEAUCHAMP, Joseph Edmond: Joseph Edmond Beauchamp, age 10 months, died 12 April 1899, buried 13 April 1899, Witness: Bernard Beauchamp, Emmanuel Garon priest. (page 138)

BEAUCHAMP, Marie Agnes: B-3, Marie Agnes Beauchamp, born 26 March 1900, baptized 27 March 1900, Bernard Beauchamp and Emma Lacerte, Godfather: Louis Dumais, Godmother: Florestine Lacerte, Emmanuel Garon priest. (page 35)

BEAUCHAMP, Marie Anne: Marie Anne Beauchamp, age 25, died 8 August 1903, C. J. Passaplan. (page 139)

BEAUCHAMP, Napoleon: B-4, Napoleon Beauchamp, born 28 May 1887, baptized 29 May 1887, son of Abraham Beauchamp and Marie Desjardins, Godfather: Louis Briere, Godmother: Josette Berard, Pierre St.Germain o.m.i. (page 13)

BEAUCHAMP, Napoleon: Napoleon Beauchamp, age 5, died 7 February 1892, buried 8 February 1892, Witness: Pierre Bruyere, Pierre St.Germain priest. (page 138)

BEAUCHAMP, Pierre: Pierre Beauchamp, age 18, died 15 August 1890, buried 16 August 1890, Witness: Louis Bruyere, Pierre St.Germain priest. (page 137)

BEAUPRE, Elise: Elise Beaupre, age 2-1/2, died 23 April 1890, buried 24 April 1890, Prudent Lapointe, Pierre

St.Germain priest. (page 137)

BEAUPRE, Florestine Edouardina: B-14, Florestine Edouardina Beaupre, born 14 July 1904, baptized 14 July 1904, daughter of Gaspard Beaupre and Florestine Piche, Godfather: Edouard Lesperance, Godmother: Veronique Chartrand, C. J. Passaplan priest. (page 45)

BEAUPRE, Gaspard Oscar: B-5, Gaspard Oscar Beaupre, born 13 June 1890, baptized 13 June 1890, son of Gaspard Beaupre and Florestine Piche, Godfather: Joseph Hamelin, Godmother: Philomene Piche, Pierre St.Germain o.m.i. (page 18)

BEAUPRE, Gaspard Oscar: B-24, Gaspard Oscar Beaupre, born 15 December 1900, baptized 16 December 1900, son of Gaspard Beaupre and Florestine Piche, Godfather: Zacharie Chartrand, Godmother: Vicoire Breland, Pierre St.Germain o.m.i.; married 24 October 1926, Sarah Delorme. (page 37)

BEAUPRE, Joseph Edouard: B-1, Joseph Edouard Beaupre, born 9 January 1881, baptized 9 January 1881, son of Gaspard Beaupre and Florestine Piche, Godfather: Jean Louis Legare, Godmother: Florestine Piche, Pierre St.Germain o.m.i. (page 1)

BEAUPRE, Josephine and Edmond LESPERANCE: M-1, Edmond Lesperance, born 15 January 1880 SFX, son of Alexandre Lesperance and Cleophee Page, married 5 January 1904, Josephine Beaupre, daughter of Gaspard Beaupre and Florestine Piche, Witness: Hormidas Granger and Alexandre Briere, C. J. Passaplan priest. (page 114)

BEAUPRE, Jules: B-18, Jules Beaupre, born 16 November 1893, baptized 25 December 1893, son of Gaspard Beaupre and Florestine Piche, Godfather: Jean Baptiste Dumais, Godmother: Vitaline Piche, A. Leuret priest. (page 23)

BEAUPRE, Louis Denis Alfred: B-5, Louis Denis Alfred Beaupre, born 23 May 1892, baptized 23 May 1892, son of Gaspard Beaupre and Florestine Piche, Godfather: Jean Chartrand, Godmother: Athalie Rose Piche, Pierre St.Germain o.m.i. (page 21)

BEAUPRE, Maria: Maria Beaupre, age 6 months, died 7 April 1900, buried 8 April 1900, Witness: Gaspard Beaupre, Emmanuel Garon priest. (page 138)

BEAUPRE, Maria Georgiana: B-3, Maria Georgiana Beaupre, born September 1898, baptized 30 October 1898, daughter of Gaspard Beaupre and Florestine Piche, Godfather: Louis Briere, Godmother: Josette Berard, Emmanuel Garon priest. (page 32)

BEAUPRE, Maria Stella: B-18, Maria Stella Beaupre, born 18 October 1899, baptized 22 October 1899, daughter of Gaspard Beaupre and Florestine Piche, Godfather: Emmanuel Garon priest, Godmother: Antonia Granger, Emmanuel Garon priest. (page 34)

BEAUPRE, Marie Anne: B-12, Marie Anne Beaupre, born 17 September 1897, baptized 16 November 1897, daughter of Gaspard Beaupre and Florestine Piche, Godfather: Joseph Lapointe, Godmother: Eleonore Ouellette, Pierre St.Germain o.m.i. (page 31)

BEAUPRE, Marie Elisabeth Elise: B-13, Marie Elisabeth Elise Beaupre, born 4 October 1887, baptized 30 October 1887, daughter of Gaspard Beaupre and Florestine Piche, Godfather: Prudent Lapointe, Godmother: Elisabeth Ouellette, Pierre St.Germain o.m.i. (page 14)

BEAUPRE, Marie: Marie Beaupre, daughter of Gaspard Beaupre, buried 23 March 1906, M. Mesnage priest V.

(page 139)

BEAUPRE, Marie Josephine: B-15, Marie Josephine Beaupre, born 14 September 1885, baptized 14 September 1885, daughter of Gaspard Beaupre and Florestine Piche, Godfather: Louis Piche, Godmother: Cecile Desmarais, Pierre St.Germain o.m.i. (page 8)

BEAUPRE, Marie Rose: Marie Rose Beaupre, age 4 months, died 28 March 1895, buried 29 March 1895, Witness: family, A. Lerch priest. (page 138)

BEAUPRE, Marie Rose Anne: B-14, Marie Rose Anne Beaupre, born 12 December 1894, baptized 15 December 1894, daughter of Gaspard Beaupre and Florestine Piche, Godfather: Albert Legare, Godmother: Justine Piche, A. Leuret priest. (page 25)

BEAUPRE, Marie Rosina: B-1, Marie Rosina Beaupre, born 6 January 1896, baptized 7 January 1896, daughter of Gaspard Beaupre and Florestine Piche, Godfather: Alexandre McGillis, Godmother: Isabelle Fagnan, A. Leuret priest. (page 28)

BEAUPRE, Oscar: Oscar Beaupre, infant, buried 24 January 1901, Witness: Gaspard Beaupre, Pierre St.Germain priest. (page 139)

BELLEGARDE, Adeline and Louis GAUDRY: M-3, Louis Gaudry, minor son of Andre Gaudry and Marie Beauchamp, married 4 June 1901, Adeline Bellegarde, minor daughter of Pierre Bellegarde and Marie Fidler, Witness: Moise Gaudry and Bernard Langer, Pierre St.Germain o.m.i. (page 114)

BELLEGARDE, Jean Baptiste: B-11, Jean Baptiste Bellegarde, born 31 July 1882, baptized 28 February 1883, son of Clovis Bellegarde and Rosine Bonneau, Godfather: Antoine Bellegarde, Godmother: Victoire Descoteaux, P. St.Germain o.m.i. (page 3)

BELLEGARDE, Marie: B-24, Marie Bellegarde, born 17 February 1883, baptized 12 September 1883, daughter of Baptiste Bellegarde and Marie Hamelin, Godfather: Jean Baptiste Amyot, Godmother: Sarah Delorme, Pierre St.Germain o.m.i. (page 4)

BELLEHUMEUR: Marie Cecile Germaine: B-9, Marie Cecile Germaine Bellehumeur, born 4 July 1894, baptized 19 August 1894, daughter of Edwin Bellehumeur and Rose Anne Turenne, Godfather: Charles Bellehumeur, Godmother: Cecile Payette, A. Leuret priest. (page 25)

BELLEROSE, Monique and Francois DUMONT: M-2, Francois Dumont son of Vital Dumont and Adelaide Gagnon, married 2 March 1883, Monique Bellerose daughter of Olivier Bellerose and Catherine Surprenant, Witness: Mathias Sansregret and Louis Dumais, Pierre St.Germain o.m.i. (page 110)

BENNETT, Flora: B-14, Flora Bennett, born 16 July 1897, baptized 19 July 1897, daughter of T. J. Bennet and Ann Dunlap, Godfather: David Bennett, Godmother: Mary Bennett, Pierre St.Germain o.m.i. (page 31)

BERGER, Marie Philomene: B-9, Marie Philomene Berger, born 18 March 1895, baptized 14 April 1895, daughter of Bernard Berger and Caroline Depousse, Godfather: Francois Lemaire, Godmother: Francoise Beston, A. Leuret priest. (page 26)

BESTON, Adele: B-4, Adele Beston, born 8 January 1897, baptized 8 March 1897, daughter of William Beston and Marie Rose Gosselin, Godfather: Joseph Bonneau, Godmother: Adele Gosselin, Pierre St.Germain o.m.i.; married 7 January 1918, Gedeon Legare. (page 30)

BESTON, Celina: B-9, Celina Beston, born 9 November 1892, baptized 27 November 1892, daughter of William Beston and Marie Rose Gosselin, Godfather: Joseph Hamelin, Godmother: Elemence Briere, Pierre St.Gemain o.m.i., married, 20 April 1910, Johnny Chartrand. (page 21)

BESTON, Clemence: B-20, Clemence Beston, born 17 June 1886, baptized 4 July 1886, daughter of William Beston and Marie Rose Gosselin, Godfather: Alexandre Gosselin, Godmother: Marie Champagne, Pierre St.Germain o.m.i. (page 11)

BESTON, Clemence: Clemence Beston, age 15, died 15 November 1891, buried 3 December 1891, Witness: Charles Champagne, Pierre St.Germain priest. (page 137)

BESTON, Joseph Emile: B-9, Joseph Emile Beston, born 30 November 1898, baptized 4 December 1898, son of William Beston and Marie Rose Gosselin, Godfather: Louis Briere, Godmother: Josette Berard, Emmanuel Garon priest. (page 32)

BESTON, Joseph Paul: B-3, Joseph Paul Beston, born 25 January 1908, baptized 25 January 1908, son of William Beston and Marie Rose Gosselin, Godmother: Rose Beston, Alphonse Lemieux priest; married 22 November 1939 Annie Fitzpatrick. (page 53)

BESTON, Josephine: B-10, Josephine Beston, born 1905, baptized _, daughter of Wililam Beston and Marie Rose Gosselin, Godfather: Edmond Lesperance, Godmother: Josephine Beaupre, C. J. Passaplan priest. (page 47)

BESTON, Julien: B-1, Julien Beston, born 30 December 1894, baptized 16 January 1895, son of William Beston and Marie Rose Gosselin, Godfather: Alexandre Gosselin, Godmother: Clemence Briere, A. Leuret priest; married 8 June 1926, Marie Rivard. (page 26)

BESTON, Marie Louise: Marie Louise Beston, age 4, died 2 December 1891, buried 3 December 1891, Witness: Patrice Gosselin, Pierre St.Germain priest. (page 137)

BESTON, Mathilda: B-3, Mathilda Beston, born 4 February 1901, baptized 17 February 1901, daughter of William Beston and Marie Rose Gosselin, Godfather: Georges Klyne, Godmother: Sarah Gosselin, Pierre St.Germain o.m.i.; married, 31 January 1918, Marius Legare. (page 38)

BESTON, Rose: B-8, Rose Beston, born 5 December 1890, baptized 7 December 1890, daughter of William Beston and Marie Rose Gosselin, Godfather: Alexander Gosselin, Pierre St.Germain, died December 1848, at Fort Qu'Appelle, married 8 April 1913, Louis Haggeyt, married 29 November 1923, E.McGillis. (page 18)

BESTON, Therese: Therese Beston, age 6, died 6 December 1891, buried 7 December 1891, Witness: Louis Larocque, Pierre St.Germain priest. (page 137)

BESTON, William: B-14, William Beston, born 25 May 1903, baptized 2 June 1903, son of William Beston and Marie Rose Gosselin, Godfather: Emmanuel Gosselin, Godmother: Emerence Gosselin, C. J. Passaplan priest; married 24 July 1924 Virginie Roy. (page 43)

BONNEAU, Anna Marie Louise: B-18, Anna Marie Louise Bonneau, born 23 August 1906, baptized 2 September 1906, daughter of Treffle Bonneau and Marie Louise Vaudry, Godfather: Joseph Gagne, Godmother: Marie Eugenie St.Hilaire, Alphonse Lemieux priest. (page 50)

BONNEAU, Cecile Blanche: B-12, Cecile Blanche Bonneau, born 22 May 1896, baptized 22 June 1896, daughter of Treffle Bonneau and Marie Louise Vaudry, Godfather: Joseph Bonneau, Godmother: Albina Bonneau, Pierre St.Germain o.m.i.; married 25 November 1915, Remy Provost. (page 29)

BONNEAU, Jean Pascal: B-5, Jean Pascal Bonneau, born 5 March 1895, baptized 10 March 1895, son of Treffle Bonneau and Marie Louise Vaudry, Godfather: Pascal Bonneau, Godmother: Albina Bonneau, A. Leuret priest; married, 3 July 1917, Estella Lavallie; married 2nd Gabrielle Dalcourt, married 16 August 1927, 3rd, Lumina Roy. (page 27)

BONNEAU, Joseph Albert: B-8, Joseph Albert Bonneau, born 4 October 1891, baptized 9 October 1892, son of Treffle Bonneau and Marie Louise Vaudry, Godfather: Pascal Bonneau, Godmother: Eugenie Bellehumeur, Pierre St.Germain. (page 21)

BONNEAU, Joseph Edgard: B-8, Joseph Edgard Bonneau, born 9 May 1905, baptized 14 May 1905, son of Treffle Bonneau and Marie Louise Vaudry, Godfather: Octave Halle, Godmother: Angele Boulianne, C. J. Dasasplan priest; married 22 May 1928 Alice Legare. (page 47)

BONNEAU, Louis: B-15, Louis Bonneau, born 17 October 1897, baptized 20 November 1897, son of Treffle Bonneau and Marie Louise Vaudry, Godfather: Louis Dumais, Godmother: Elisa Caplette, Pierre St.Germain o.m.i.; married 31 December 1928, Marie Justine Gaudry. (page 31)

BONNEAU, Marie Antoinette: B-1, Marie Antoinette Bonneau, born 12 January 1903, baptized 13 January 1903, son of Treffle Bonneau and Marie Louise Vaudry, Godfather: Edouard Beaupre, Godmother: Florestine Piche, C. J. Passaplan priest; married 11 November 1921 Henri Audette. (page 42)

BONNEAU, Marie Celina Albertine: B-13, Marie Celina Albertine Bonneau, born 14 April 1908, baptized 16 April 1908, daughter of Treffle Bonneau and Marie Louise Vaudry, Godfather: Jean Bonneau, Godmother: Blanche Bonneau, Alphonse Lemieux priest, married 17 May 1927 Romeo Rodrique. (page 54)

BONNEAU, Marie Corinne: B-6, Marie Corinne Bonneau, born 11 April 1900, baptized 12 April 1900, daughter of Treffle Bonneau and Marie Louise Vaudry, Godfather: Prudent Lapointe, Godmother: Elisabeth Ouellette, Emmanuel Garon priest, married, 14 January 1919 [?], Trevie Granger. (page 35)

BONNEAU, Paschal: Paschal Bonneau, age 47, died 28 January 1910, buried 1 February 1910, Alphonse Lemieux priest. (page 140)

BOTINEAU, Angelique: Angelique Botineau, died 14 September 1903, buried 16 September 1903, C. J. Passaplan. (page 139)

BOTINEAU, Eyenor: Eyenor Botineau, age 19, died 5 June 1889, 6 June 1889, Witness: Joseph Lapointe, Pierre St.Germain priest. (page 137)

BOTINEAU, Francois and Therese MCGILLIS: M-1, Francois Botineau, married 7 January 1891, Therese McGillis, Witness: Joseph Short and Francois Lafournaise, Pierre St.Germain o.m.i. (page 112)

BOTINEAU, Francois: Francois Botineau, infant of Joseph Bottineau, age 4, buried 7 December 1908, Alphonse Lemieux, priest. (page 139)

BOTINEAU, Francois Xavier: B-8, Francois Xavier Botineau, born 22 April 1904, baptized 26 April 1904, son of Joseph Botineau and Adelaide Thomas, Godfather: Louis McGillis, Godmother: Marguerite Thomas, C. J. Passaplan priest. (page 45)

BOTINEAU, Joseph: Joseph Botineau, age 6 months, died 28 November 1900, buried 30 November 1900, Witness: Joseph Botineau, Pierre St.Germain priest. (page 138)

BOTINEAU, Joseph: Joseph Botineau, age 23, died 17 October 1916, buried, 18 October 1916, Alphonse Lemieux priest. (page 142)

BOTINEAU, Joseph and Adelaide THOMAS: M-3, Joseph Botineau, son of Joseph Botineau and Louise Vallee, married 7 November 1895, Adelaide Thomas, daughter of Francois Thomas and Marie Adele _, Witness: Albert Legare and Albert Beauchamp, Albert Leuret priest. (page 113)

BOTINEAU, Joseph Alfred: B-5, Joseph Alfred Botineau, born 7 April 1900, baptized 7 April 1900, Francois Botineau and Therese McGillis, Godfather: Louis Briere, Godmother: Josette Berard, Emmanuel Garon priest; married 25 April 1922, Adele Gosselin. (page 35)

BOTINEAU, Joseph Alfred: B-10, Joseph Alfred Botineau, born 29 April 1900, baptized 29 April 1900, son of Joseph Botineau and Adelaide Thomas, Godfather: Clement Lacerte, Godmother: Rosalie Granger, Emmanuel Garon priest. (page 36)

BOTINEAU, Joseph St.Pierre: B-3, Joseph St.Pierre Botineau, born December 1898, baptized 15 February 1899, son of Joseph Botineau and Adelaide Thomas, Godfather: Louis Dumont, Godmother: Philomene Thomas, Emmanuel Garon priest. (page 33)

BOTINEAU, Joseph Thomas: B-6, Joseph Thomas Botineau, born 6 March 1893, baptized 7 March 1893, son of Francois Botineau and Therese McGillis, Godfather: Alexandre McGillis, Godmother: Marie Jeannotte, Pierre St.Germain o.m.i. (page 22)

BOTINEAU, Josette and Joseph SHORT: M-3, Joseph Short, married 30 May 1887, Josette Botineau, Witness: Louis Piche and Joseph Botineau, Pierre St.Germain o.m.i. (page 111)

BOTINEAU, Josette: Josette Botineau, wife of Joseph Short, age 78, buried 18 May 1914, V. Rabard priest. (page 141)

BOTINEAU, Louis: Louis Botinoh [Botineau], age 1, died 20 April 1899, buried 21 April 1899, Witness: Francois Botinoh, Emmanuel Garon priest. (page 138)

BOTINEAU, Louis Eugene: B-1, Louis Eugene Botineau, born 2 February 1898, baptized 4 May 1898, Francois Botineau and Marie Therese McGillis, Godfather: Gregoire McGillis, Godmother: Eleonore Ouellette, Pierre St.Germain o.m.i. (page 32)

BOTINEAU, Marie: B-11, Marie Botineau, born 26 May 1905, baptized 1 June 1905, daughter of unknown and Isabelle Botineau, Godfather: Louis Laplante, Godmother: Virginie Fleury, C. J. Passaplan priest. (page 48)

BOTINEAU, Marie Antoinette: B-5, Marie Antoinette Botineau, born 23 February 1906, baptized 25 February 1906, daughter of Joseph Botineau and Marie Adelaide Thomas, Godfather: Antoine Caplette, Godmother: Nathalie Thomas, M. Mesnage vic. (page 49)

BOTINEAU, Marie Celina: B-24, Marie Celina Botineau (twin), born 5 December 1903, baptized 6 December 1903, daughter of Francois Botineau and Marie Therese McGillis, Godfather: Jean Marie McGillis, Godmother: Adele Parent, C. J. Passaplan priest. (page 44)

St.Ignace Parish of Willow Bunch, Saskatchewan
1882-1910, Baptisms, Marriages and Burials

BOTINEAU, Marie Julie: B-13, Marie Julie Botineau, born 13 September 1895, baptized 15 September 1895, daughter of Francois Botineau and Therese McGillis, Godfather: Theophile McGillis, Godmother: Josette Gosselin, A. Leuret priest; married, 15 November 1918, Alfred Bruneau. (page 27)

BOTINEAU, Marie Julie: Marie Julie Botineau, age 8, died 19 December 1886, buried 21 December 1886, Witness: Elzear Botineau, Pierre St.Germain priest. (page 137)

BOTINEAU, Marie Louise BOTINEAU: B-2, Marie Louise Botineau, born 5 December 1896, baptized 3 March 1897, daughter of Joseph Botineau and Adelaide Thomas, Godfather: Joseph Botineau, Godmother: Louise Vallee, Pierre St.Germain o.m.i. (page 30)

BOTINEAU, Romuald: B-23, Romuald Botineau (twin), born 5 December 1903, baptized 6 December 1903, son of Francois Botineau and Marie Therese McGillis, Godfather: Narcisse Lacerte, Godmother: Seraphine Ouellete, C. J. Passaplan priest. (page 44)

BOTINEAU, Rosalie: B-14, Rosalie Botineau, born 15 July 1902, baptized 16 July 1902, daughter of Joseph Botineau and Adelaide Thomas, Godfather: Elzear Botineau, Godmother: Rosalie Morin, C. J. Passaplan priest. (page 41)

BOTINEAU, St.Pierre: St.Pierre Botinoh [Botineau], age 3 months, died 22 February 1899, buried 28 February 1899, Witness: Joseph Botinoh, Emmanuel Garon priest. (page 138)

BOTINEAU, Virginie: B-17, Virginie Botineau, born 22 October 1891, baptized 24 October 1891, daughter of Francois Botineau and Therese McGillis, Godfather: Elzear Botineau, Godmother: Isabella St.Pierre, Pierre St.Germain o.m.i. (page 20)

BOTINEAU, Virginie: Virginie Botineau, age 7 months, died 14 May 1892, buried 14 May 1896, Witness: Isidore Ouellette, Pierre St.Germain priest. (page 138)

BOULIANNE, Gelida and Norbert PARKER: M-3, Norbert Parker, son of Bernard Joseph Parker and Marie Anne Ward (Anglican), married 9 August 1909, Gelida Boulianne, daughter of Rieul Boulianne and Sarah Simard, Witness: Octave Rolli and Pascal Bonneau, Alphonse Lemieux priest. (page 116)

BOXEUR, Adele: B-8, Adele Boxeur, born 12 April 1895, baptized 14 April 1895, daughter of Francois Boxeur and Elise McGillis, Godfather: Louis R. McGillis, Godmother: Mathilde McGillis, A. Leuret priest; married 7 August 1917, Georges Lecoine. (page 26)

BOXEUR, Antoine: B-17, Antoine Boxeur, born 16 July 1909, baptized 18 July 1909, son of Francois Boxeur and Elise McGillis, Godfather: Antoine Caplete, Godmother: Nathalie Trottier, Alphonse Lemieux priest. (page 58)

BOXEUR, Francois: B-5, Francois Boxeur, born 3 May 1889, baptized 5 May 1889, son of Francois Boxeur and Elise McGillis, Godfather: Alexandre McGillis, Godmother: Isabelle Faynan, Pierre St.Germain o.m.i.; married 13 May 1913, Marie Louise Lapointe. (page 16)

BOXEUR, Francois: Francois Boxeur, husband of Elise McGillis, age 48, buried 4 December 1912, J. A. Auteuel priest. (page 140)

BOXEUR, Francois and Elise MCGILLIS: M-4, Francois Boxeur, son of Joseph Boxeur and Julie Sauteuse, married 7 June 1886, Elise McGillis, daughter of Modeste McGillis and Isabelle Poitras, Witness: Andre Gaudry and Isidore

Ouellette, Pierre St.Germain o.m.i. (page 111)

BOXEUR, Joseph Albert: B-10, Joseph Albert Boxeur, born 20 December 1898, baptized 22 December 1898, Francois Boxeur and Elise McGillis, Godfather: Alexandre McGillis, Godmother: Marie Jeannotte, Emmanuel Garon priest (page 32)

BOXEUR, Joseph Albert: Joseph Albert Boxer, age 1 month, died 27 January 1899, buried 28 January 1899, Witness: Francois Boxer, Emmanuel Garon priest. (page 138)

BOXEUR, Josephine: B-4, Josephine Boxeur, born 15 February 1893, baptized 15 February 1893, daughter of Francois Boxeur and Elise McGillis, Godfather: Joseph Short, Godmother: Josette Botineau, Pierre St.Germain o.m.i., married 9 January 1912, Magloire Gosselin. (page 22)

BOXEUR, Louis: B-3, Louis Boxeur, born 28 February 1897, baptized 6 March 1897, son of Francois Boxeur and Elise McGillis, Godfather: Alphonse Langer, Godmother: Marie Page, Pierre St.Germain o.m.i. (page 30)

BOXEUR, Marie Adelaide: B-2, Marie Adelaide Boxeur, born 28 January 1900, baptized 31 January 1900, daughter of Francois Boxeur and Elise McGillis, Godfather: Joseph Botineau, Godmother: Adelaide Thomas, Emmanuel Garon priest. (page 35)

BOXEUR, Marie Marguerite: B-1, Marie Marguerite Boxeur, born 1 January 1906, baptized 5 January 1906, daughter of Francois Boxeur and Elise McGillis, Godfather: Louis Dumais, Godmother: Marie Roy, Alphonse Lemieux priest. (page 49)

BOXEUR, Marie Rose: B-19, Marie Rose Boxeur, born 3 September 1903, baptized 3 September 1903, daughter of Francois Boxeur and Elise McGillis, Godfather: Prudent Lapointe, Godmother: Elisabeth Ouellette, C. J. Passaplan priest. (page 43)

BOXEUR, Vitaline: B-3, Vitaline Boxeur, born 3 April 1891, baptized 4 April 1891, daughter of Francois Boxeur and Elise McGillis, Godfather: Modeste McGillis, Godmother: Isabelle Poitras, Pierre St.Germain o.m.i. (page 19)

BOYER, Marie Emelie: B-12, Marie Emelie Boyer, born 15 December 1882, baptized 27 December 1882, daughter of Ambroise Boyer and Emerence Briere, Godfather: Norbert Boyer, Godmother: Felicite Patenaude, Pierre St.Germain o.m.i. (page 2)

BRELAND, Francois: B-8, Francois Breland, born 23 May 1896, baptized 15 June 1896, son of Pascal Breland and Elisa Boyer, Godfather: Jean Baptiste Trottier, Godmother: Rosalie Trottier, Pierre St.Germain o.m.i. (page 28)

BRELAND, John: B-9, John Breland, born 8 June 1891, baptized 10 June 1891, son of John Breland and Rose Ouellette, Godfather: Alexandre McGillis, Godmother: Rose Ouellette, Pierre St.Germain o.m.i. (page 19)

BRELAND, Marie Amelie: B-23, Marie Amelie Breland, born 18 May 1886, baptized 20 July 1886, Zacharie Breland and Marie Trottier, Godfather: Patrice Trottier, Godmother: Marie Rose Trottier, Pierre St.Germain o.m.i. (page 12)

BRIANT, Joseph Alexandre: B-14, Joseph Alexandre Briant, born 29 August 1905, baptized 3 September 1905, son of Alexandre Briant and Marie Langer, Godfather: Louis Dumais, Godmother: Elisa Caplette, Alphonse Lemieux priest. (page 48)

BRIEN, Josephine: B-20, Josephine Brien, born 21 September 1903, baptized 28 September 1903, daughter of

St.Ignace Parish of Willow Bunch, Saskatchewan
1882-1910, Baptisms, Marriages and Burials

Alexandre Brien and Helene Landry, Godfather: Ambroise Chartrand, Godmother: Francoise Landry, C. J. Passaplan priest. (page 43)

BRIERE, Celina and Zacharie PICHE: M-1, Zacharie Piche, son of Louison and Cecile Desmarais, married 15 January 1895, Celina Briere, daughter of Jeremie Briere and Lisa Allary, Witness: Albert Legare and Johnny Chartrand, Albert Leuret priest. (page 113)

BRIERE, Clemence and Alexandre GOSSELIN: M-1, Alexandre Gosselin, son of Alexandre Gosselin and Marie Champagne, married 3 January 1887, Clemence Briere, daughter of Louis Briere and Joseph Berard, Witness: Pierre Briere and Francois Lafournaise, Pierre St.Germain o.m.i. (page 111)

BRIERE, Damase : B-6, Damase Briere, born 20 September 1890, baptized 25 September 1890, son of Louis Briere and Josette Berard, Godfather: Alexandre Gosselin Jr., Godmother: Clemence Briere, Pierre St.Germain o.m.i. (page 18)

BRIERE, Emelie and Alexandre GOSSELIN: M-3, Alexandre Gosselin, son of Antonie Gosselin and Francoise Delorme, married 1 May 1893, Emilie Briere, daughter of Louis Briere and Josette Berard, Witness: Theophile McGillis and Pierre Briere, Pierre St.Germain o.m.i. (page 112)

BRIERE, Ernestine and Louis DUMAIS: M-3, Louis Dumais, widower of Elisa Caplette, married 3 November 1908, Ernestine Briere, daughter of Louison Briere and Josette Berard, Witness: Gaspard Beaupre and Zacharie Chartrand, Alphonse Lemieux priest. (page 115)

BRIERE, Guillaume: B-31, Guillaume Briere, born 18 June 1883, baptized 23 September 1883, son of Jean Baptiste Briere and Marie Emmery, Godfather: Louis Piche, Cecile Desmarais, Pierre St.Germain o.m.i. (page 5)

BRIERE, Joseph: B-27, Joseph Briere, born 25 August 1886, baptized 29 August 1886, son of Louis Briere and Josette Berard, Godfather: Joseph Langer, Godmother: Marie Rose McGillis, Pierre St.Germain o.m.i. (page 12)

BRIERE, Joseph Angus: B-4, Joseph Angus Briere, born 11 February 1903, baptized 12 February 1903, son of Pierre Briere and Marie Caplette, Godfather: Alexandre Briere, Godmother: Marie Hamelin, C. J. Passaplan priest. (page 42)

BRIERE, Joseph Noel: Joseph Noel Briere, age 4 days, buried 16 December 1910, A. Lemieux priest. (page 140)

BRIERE, Joseph Thomas: B-32, Joseph Thomas Briere, born 9 November 1908, born 12 November 1908, son of Pierre Briere and Marie Caplette, Godfather: Joseph Anderson, Godmother: Isabella Contois, Alphonse Lemieux priest; married 16 June 1928 Milda Ivy Loreene Foulds. (page 56)

BRIERE, Josephine: Josephine Briere, infant of Pierre Briere, age 15 months, buried 23 February 1906, M. Mesnage priest V. (page 139)

BRIERE, Louis Alcide: B-4, Louis Alcide Briere, born 6 February 1902, baptized 22 February 1902, son of Pierre Briere and Marie Caplette, Godfather: Louis Briere, Godmother: Josette Berard, Pierre St.Germain o.mi.; married Meadow Lake, 22 February 1927 Rose Malboeuf. (page 40)

BRIERE, Louise: B-1, Louise Briere, born 8 January 1904, baptized 31 January 1904, daughter of Alexandre Briere and Marie Beston, Godfather: Joseph Laplante, Godmother: Louise Leveille, C. J. Passaplan priest. (page 44)

BRIERE, Louison: Louison Brierre, age 60, buried 24 January 1906, Alphonse Lemieux, priest. (page 139)

BRIERE, Marie: B-19, Marie Briere, born 28 October 1904, baptized 30 October 1904, daughter of Pierre Briere and Marie Caplette, Godfather: Jean Baptiste Caplette, Godmother: Flora _, C. J. Passaplan priest. (page 46)

BRIERE, Marie and Bernard HAMELIN: M-2, Bernard Hamelin, son of Moise Hamelin and Isabelle Wichcoupe, married 1 February 1887, Marie Briere, daughter of Louis Briere and Josette Berard, Witness: Louis Piche and Louis Briere, Pierre St.Germain o.m.i. (page 111)

BRIERE, Marie Eugenie: Marie Eugenie Briere, age 2 days, buried 15 December 1910, A. Lemieux priest. (page 140)

BRIERE, Marie Therese and Alexandre GOSSELIN: M-1, Alexandre Gosselin, son of Alexandre Gosselin and Marie Champagne, married 8 August 1903, Marie Therese Briere, C. J. Passaplan priest. (page 114)

BRIERE, Marie Therese: Therese Briere, spouse of Alex Gosselin, age 30, buried 26 October 1910, A. Lemieux priest. (page 140)

BRIERE, Napoleon: B-6, Napoleon Briere, born 29 December 1888, baptized 30 December 1888, son of Louis Briere and Josette Berard, Godfather: Louis Piche, Godmother: Cecile Desmarais, Pierre St.Germain o.m.i. (page 15)

BRIERE, Pierre: B-19, Pierre Briere, born 9 September 1906, baptized 17 September 1906, son of Pierre Briere and Marie Caplette, Godfather: Joseph Morin, Godmother: Elisa Desjarlais, Alphonse Lemieux priest. (page 50)

BRIERE, Pierre and Marie CAPLETTE: M-2, Pierre Briere, adult son of Louis Briere and Josette Berard, married 7 May 1901, Marie Caplette, minor daughter of Jean Baptiste Caplette and Anastasie Morin, Witness: Louis Dumais and Alexandre Briere, Pierre St.Germain o.m.i. (page 113)

BRUNING, Anna: Anna Bruning, age 42, buried 8 March 1910, Alphonse Lemieux priest. (page 140)

BRUYERE, Ambroise: Ambroise Bruyere, age 12, died 24 June 1889, buried 24 June 1889, Witness: Louis Roy, Pierre St.Germain priest. (page 137)

BRUYERE, Jeremie: Jeremie Bruyere, age 37, buried 26 August 1891, Witness: Louis Laroque, Pierre St.Germain priest. (page 137)

BRUYERE, Jerome: Jerome Bruyere, age _, died 6 June 1890, buried 7 June 1890, Witness: Bernard Hamelin, Pierre St.Germain priest. (page 137)

BURNS, Beatrice: B-15, Beatrice Burns, born 21 March 1895, Moose Jaw, baptized 4 October 1895, daughter of John Burns and Mary _, A. Leuret priest (page 27)

BURNS, Benjamin: B-13, Benjamin Burns, born 4 May 1906, baptized 13 June 1909, son of Benjamin Burns and Helene Blum, Godfather: Patrice Caplette, Alphonse Lemieux priest. (page 58)

BURNS, John Walter: B-18, John Walter Burns, born 3 May 1896, baptized 10 December 1897, son of John Burns and Mary Crossby, Godfather: Martin Burns, Godmother: Maria Burns, Pierre St.Germain o.m.i. (page 31)

BURNS, Marie Helene: B-11, Marie Helene Burns, born 1 March 1909, baptized 13 June 1909, daughter of Benjamin Burns and Helene Blum, Godfather: Joseph Beausolul, Alphonse Lemieux priest. (page 58)

BURNS, Lawrence John: B-12, Lawrence John Burns, born 28 December 1907, baptized 13 June 1909, son of Benjamin Burns and Helene Blum, Godfather: A. P. Beausolul, Alphonse Lemieux priest. (page 58)

CANELLE, William: B-10, William Canelle [Quesnelle], born 25 April 1885, baptized 25 May 1885, son of Jules Canelle [Quesnelle] and Rachel McKay, Godfather: Alexis Pelletier, Godmother: Elisa McLeod, Pierre St.Germain o.m.i. (page 7)

CAPLESSE, Francois: Francois Capelesse, age 9, died 15 July 1885, buried 16 July 1885, Witness: Louis Dumais, Pierre St.Germain priest. (page 137)

CAPLETTE, Albert: B-2, Albert Caplette, born 3 March 1892, baptized 6 March 1892, son of Francois Caplette and Elise Gosselin, Godfather: Jean Baptiste Caplette, Godmother: Adele Gosselin, Pierre St.Germain o.m.i. (page 21)

CAPLETTE: Alexandre: Alexandre Caplette, son of Antoine Caplette, age 18 months, died 12 August 1907, buried 13 August 1907, J. A. Magnan priest. (page 139)

CAPLETTE, Alfred: B-19, Alfred Caplette, born 9 July 1908, baptized 12 July 1908, son of Antoine Caplette and Nathalie Trottier, Godfather: Louis Roy, Godmother: Marguerite Sauve, A. Lemieux priest. (page 55)

CAPLETTE, Alfred: Alfred Caplette, son of Antoine Caplette, age 1 month, buried 10 August 1908, Alphonse Lemieux priest. (page 139)

CAPLETTE, Ambroise: B-23, Ambroise Caplette, born 8 December 1904, baptized 15 December 1904, son of Francois Caplette and Elise Gosselin, Godfather: Alexandre Gosselin, Godmother: Therese Gosselin, C. J. Passaplan priest. (page 46)

CAPLETTE, Antoine and Athalie TROTTIER: M-1, Antoine Caplette, son of Antoine Caplette and Seraphine Houle, married 13 February 1893, Athalie Trottier, daughter of Jean Baptiste Trottier and Rose McGillis, Witness: Napoleon McGillis and Theophile McGillis, Pierre St.Germain o.m.i. (page 112)

CAPLETTE, Athalie: Athalie Caplette, age 2, died 2 November 1896, buried 3 November 1896, Witness: Louis Bruyere, Pierre St.Germain priest. (page 138)

CAPLETTE, Bruno: B-35, Bruno Caplette, born 1879, baptized 8 October 1883, son of infidel Sioux, Godfather: Louis Dumais, Godmother: Eloize Caplette, Pierre St.Germain o.m.i. (page 5)

CAPLETTE, Eliza: Eliza Caplette, age 61, Witness: Louis Dumais, buried 8 February 1907, Alphonse Lemieux priest. (page 139)

CAPLETTE, Francois: B-17, Francois Caplette, born 30 September 1900, baptized 7 October 1900, son of Francois Caplette and Elise Gosselin, Godfather: Francois Gosselin, Godmother: Helene Gosselin, Pierre St.Germain o.m.i. (page 36)

CAPLETTE, Francois: Francois Caplette, age 2 months, died 6 December 1900, buried 7 December 1900, Witness: Francois Caplette, Pierre St.Germain priest. (page 139)

CAPLETTE, Helene CONTOIS (CAPLETTE): Helene Contois, age 49, buried 18 December 1909, Alphonse Lemieux priest. (page 140)

CAPLETTE, J. Emmanuel: B-13, J. Emmanuel Caplette, born 11 June 1906, baptized 17 June 1906, son of Francois Caplette and Elise Gosselin, Godfather: Emmanuel Gosselin, Godmother: Rose Beston, Alphonse Lemieux priest; married, 11 February 1930 Marie Elisabeth Lapointe. (page 50)

CAPLETTE, Jean: B-30, Jean Caplette, born 15 October 1886, baptized 31 October 1886, son of Jean Caplette and Anastasie Morin, Godfather: Antoine Morin, Godmother: Eliza Desjarlais, Pierre St.Germain o.m.i. (page 12)

CAPLETTE, Jean: Jean Capplette, age 3, died 14 December 1889, buried 15 December 1889, Witness: Louis Dumais, Pierre St.Germain priest. (page 137)

CAPLETTE, Jean: B-2, Jean Caplette, born 14 January 1893, baptized 15 January 1893, son of Paul Caplette and Justine Poitras, Godfather: Jean Caplette, Godmother: Marie St.Arnaud, Pierre St.Germain o.m.i. (page 22)

CAPLETTE, Joseph: Joseph Caplette, age 1 day, died 22 August 1899, buried 24 August 1899, Witness: Francois Caplette, Emmanuel Garon priest. (page 138)

CAPLETTE, Joseph Napoleon: B-18, Joseph Napoleon Caplette, born 26 August 1903, baptized 31 August 1903, son of Francois Caplette and Elise Gosselin, Godfather: Napoleon Rainville, Godmother: Philomene Klyne, C. J. Passaplan priest. (page 43)

CAPLETTE, Jules: B-15, Jules Caplette, born 20 September 1891, baptized 21 September 1891, son of Paul Caplette and Justine Poitras, Godfather: Napoleon Lafournaise, Godmother: Therese McGillis, Pierre St.Germain o.m.i. (page 20)

CAPLETTE, Jules: Jules Cappelette, age 6 months, died 20 March 1892, buried 21 March 1892, Witness: Louis Roy, Pierre St.Germain priest. (page 138)

CAPLETTE, Louis Antoine: B-2, Louis Antoine Caplette, born 3 February 1894, baptized 4 February 1894, son of Antoine Caplette and Athalie Trottier, Godfather: Louis Dumais, Godmother: Elise Caplette, A. Leuret priest; married 20 May 1920, Adele Beston. (page 24)

CAPLETTE, Louise: B-10, Louise Caplette, born 29 April 1902, baptized 4 May 1902, daughter of Francois Roy and Elise Gosselin, Pierre St.Germain o.m.i. (page 40)

CAPLETTE, Marie and Pierre BRIERE: M-2, Pierre Briere, adult son of Louis Briere and Josette Berard, married 7 May 1901, Marie Caplette, minor daughter of Jean Baptiste Caplette and Anastasie Morin, Witness: Louis Dumais and Alexandre Briere, Pierre St.Germain o.m.i. (page 113)

CAPLETTE, Marie Christine: B-7, Marie Christine Caplette, born 28 March 1895, born 3 April 1895, daughter of Paul Caplette and Christine Poitras, Godfather: Louis Roy, Godmother: Marguerite Sauve, A. Leuret priest. (page 26)

CAPLETTE, Marie Josephine: B-20, Marie Josephine Caplette, born 3 December 1907, baptized 4 December 1907, son of Francois Caplette and Elise Gosselin, Godfather: Georges Klyne, Godmother: Marie Rose Gosselin (dame W. Beston), Alphonse Lemieux priest. (page 53)

CAPLETTE, Marie Josephine: Marie Josephine Caplette, infant of Francois Caplette, age 1, buried 15 June 1909, Alphonse Lemieux priest. (page 139)

CAPLETTE, Marie Madeleine: B-12, Marie Madeleine Caplette, born 4 April 1886, baptized 22 April 1886,

St.Ignace Parish of Willow Bunch, Saskatchewan
1882-1910, Baptisms, Marriages and Burials

daughter of Paul Caplette and Christine Poitras, Godfather: Louis Dumais, Godmother: Elisa Caplette, Pierre St.Germain o.m.i. (page 11)

CAPLETTE, Marie Marguerite: B-5, Marie Marguerite Caplette, born 13 January 1899, baptized 15 February 1899, daughter of Antoine Caplette and Athalie Trottier, Godfather: Alexandre McGillis, Godmother: Marie Jeannotte, Emmanuel Garon priest. (page 33)

CAPLETTE, Marie Marguerite: Marie Caplette, age 4 months, died 25 May 1899, buried 26 May 1899, Witness: Antoine Caplette, Emmanuel Garon priest. (page 138)

CAPLETTE, Marie Rose: B-17, Marie Rose Caplette, born 8 November 1896, baptized 15 November 1896, daughter of Francois Caplette and Elise Gosselin, Godfather: Napoleon McGillis, Godmother: Isabelle Fagnan, Pierre St.Germain o.m.i. (page 29)

CAPLETTE, Marie Rose: Marie Rose Caplette, age 3 months, died 2 February 1897, buried 3 March 1897, Witness: Gregoire McGillis, Pierre St.Germain priest. (page 138)

CAPLETTE, Marie Sophie: B-16, Marie Sophie Caplette, born 9 November 1901, baptized 17 November 1901, daughter of Antoine Caplette and Athalie Trottier, Godfather: Napoleon Rainville, Godmother: Florestine Lacerte, Pierre St.Germain o.m.i.; married 11 February 1918 Jean Marie McGillis. (page 39)

CAPLETTE, Nathalie Rose: B-13, Nathalie Rose Caplette, born 18 November 1894, baptized 15 December 1894, daughter of Francois Caplette and Elise Gosselin, Godfather: Jean Louis Gosselin, Godmother: Nathalie Trottier, A. Leuret priest. (page 25)

CAPLETTE, Patrice: B-7, Patrice Caplette, born 31 March 1896, baptized 31 March 1896, son of Antoine Caplette and Athalie Trottier, Godfather: Hilaire Rainville, Godmother: Seraphine Houle, A. Leuret priest. (page 28)

CAPLETTE, Pierre Tobie: B-13, Pierre Tobie Caplette, born 31 May 1900, baptized 2 June 1900, son of Antoine Caplette and Athalie Trottier, Jean Baptiste Fagnan, Godmother: Genevieve Fagnan, Pierre St.Germain o.m.i. (page 36)

CAPLETTE, Roger: Roger Cappellette, age 3, died December 1893, buried 23 February 1894, Witness: Narcisse Lacerte, A. Lerch, priest. (page 138)

CAPLETTE, Rose Anna: B-3, Rosina (Rose Anna) Caplette, born 12 February 1904, baptized 28 February 1908, daughter of Francois [Antoine] Caplette and Nathalie Trottier, Godfather: Antoine Gosselin, Godmother: Helene Piche, C. J. Passaplan priest married 10 January 1923 Louis Balaux. (page 44)

CAPLETTE, Tobie: Tobie Caplette, age 3 months, died 21 September 1900, buried 22 September 1900, Witness: Antoine Caplette, Pierre St.Germain priest. (page 138)

CARDINAL, Marie Vitaline: B-3, Marie Vitaline Cardinal, born 19 January 1883, baptized 26 January 1883, daughter of Charles Cardinal and Josette Desmarais, Godfather: Louis Piche, Godmother: Cecile Desmarais, Pierre St.Germain o.m.i. (page 2)

CARDINAL, Octavie and Isidore AMYOTTE: M-3, Isidore Amyotte, son of Joseph Amyotte and Madeleine Hamelin, married 11 February 1884, Octavie Cardinal, daughter of Charles Cardinal and Josette Desmarais, Witness: Joseph Lapointe and Thadse Ouellette, Pierre St.Germain o.m.i. (page 110)

17

St.Ignace Parish of Willow Bunch, Saskatchewan
1882-1910, Baptisms, Marriages and Burials

CARRUFEL, Gaspard Oscar: B-32, Gaspard Oscar Carrufel, born 24 September 1883, baptized 26 September 1883, son of Maxime Carrufel and Marie Desjarlais, Godfather: Gaspard Beaupre, Godmother: Florestine Piche, Pierre St.Germain o.m.i. (page 5)

CHAMPAGNE, Alfred: B-1, Alfred Champagne, born 15 February 1891, baptized 16 February 1891, son of Charles Champagne and Marie Ouellette, Godfather: Jean Baptiste Dumais, Godmother: Eleonore Ouellette, Pierre St.Germain o.m.i. (page 19)

CHAMPAGNE, Charles and Marie OUELLETTE: M-1, Charles Champagne married 6 January 1883 Marie Ouellette, Witness: Joseph Lapointe and Joseph Short, Pierre St.Germain o.m.i. (page 110)

CHAMPAGNE, Marie Athalie: B-5, Marie Athalie Champagne, born 8 April 1885, baptized 16 April 1885, daughter of Charles Champagne and Marie Ouellette, Godfather: Ambroise Ouellette, Godmother: Marie Botineau, Pierre St.Germain o.m.i. (page 6)

CHAMPAGNE, Marie Isabelle: B-2, Marie Isabelle Champagne, born 12 December 1883, baptized 17 January 1884, daughter of Charles Champagne and Marie Ouellette, Godfather: Francois Ouellette, Godfather: Eloize Ouellette, Pierre St.Germain o.m.i. (page 6)

CHAMPAGNE, Marie Ouellette: Marie Ouellette [?] Champagne, died 2 February 1895, buried 3 February 1895, Witness: family, A. Lerch priest. (page 138)

CHAMPAGNE, Marie Philomene: B-12, Marie Philomene Champagne, born 27 July 1887, baptized 30 October 1887, daughter of Charles Champagne and Marie Ouellette, Godfather: David Langer, Godmother: Emerise Lafournaise, Pierre St.Germain o.m.i. (page 14)

CHAMPAGNE, Marie Virginie: B-6, Marie Virginie Champagne, born 5 November 1882, baptized 5 December 1882, daughter of Ambroise Champagne and Judith Frederic, Godfather: Gabriel Hamelin, Godmother: Julie Amyot, Pierre St.Germain o.m.i. (page 1)

CHAMPAGNE, Rose: B-11, Rose Champagne, born 15 December 1892, baptized 18 December 1892, daughter of Charles Champagne and Marie Ouellette, Godfather: Bernard Langer, Godmother: Helene Dumais, Pierre St.Germain o.m.i. (page 22)

CHARBONNEAU, Marie Rose: Marie Rose Charbonneau, age 2, died 22 July 1886, buried 10 January 1886, Witness: Antoine Cappelesse, Pierre St.Germain priest. (page 137)

CHARBONNEAU, Patrice: Patrice Charbonneu, age 22, died 5 June 1882 [sic], buried 10 January 1887, Witness: Joseph Lapointe, Pierre St.Germain priest. (page 137)

CHARTRAND, Alfred Bernard: B-11, Alfred Bernard Chartrand, born 11 November 1897, baptized 14 November 1897, son of Johnny Chartrand and Athalie Piche, Godfather: Bernard Langer, Godmother: Eleonore Ouellette, Pierre St.Germain o.m.i. (page 31)

CHARTRAND, Clement: B-17, Clement Chartrand, born 21 November 1887, baptized 23 November 1887, son of Zacharie Chartrand and Victoire Breland, Godfather: Isidore Ouellette, Godmother: Josette Langer, Pierre St.Germain o.m.i. (page 14)

CHARTRAND, Clement: Clement Chartrand, age 4, died 17 December 1891, buried 18 December 1891, Witness: Jean Chartrand, Pierre St.Germain priest. (page 137)

CHARTRAND, Gabriel: B-21, Gabriel Chartrand, born 11 October 1903, baptized 13 October 1903, son of Johnny Chartrand and Marie Rose Piche, Godfather: Ambroise Chartrand, Godmother: Francoise Landry, C. J. Passaplan priest. (page 43)

CHARTRAND, Jean: B-5, Jean Chartrand, born 23 May 1891, baptized 30 May 1891, Johnny Chartrand and Nathalie Piche, Godfather: Zacharie Chartrand, Godmother: Victoire Breland, Pierre St.Germain o.m.i.; married, 26 April 1910, Celina Beston. (page 19)

CHARTRAND, Jean Pierre: B-6, Jean Pierre Chartrand, born 19 February 1903, baptized 20 February 1903, son of Ambroise Chartrand and Francois Landry, Godfather: Johnny Chartrand, Godmother: Marie Rose Chartrand, C. J. Passaplan priest. (page 42)

CHARTRAND, Joseph: B-10, Joseph Chartrand, born 11 August 1889, baptized 11 August 1889, son of Zacharie Chartrand and Victoire Breland, Godfather: Louis Piche, Godmother: Cecile Desmarais, Pierre St.Germain o.m.i. (page 16)

CHARTRAND, Joseph: Joseph Chartrand, age 2, died 19 December 1891, buried 20 December 1891, Witness: Jean Chartrand, Pierre St.Germain priest. (page 137)

CHARTRAND, Joseph: Joseph Chartrand, age 1 month, died 8 February 1899, buried 9 February 1899, Witness: Johnny Chartrand, Emmanuel Garon priest. (page 138)

CHARTRAND, Joseph: Joseph Chartrand, age 10 months, buried 25 September 1900, Witness: John Chartrand, Pierre St.Germain priest. (page 138)

CHARTRAND, Joseph Arsene: B-14, Joseph Arsene Chartrand, born 3 August 1893, baptized 6 October 1893, son of Jean Chartrand and Athalie Piche, Godfather: Joseph Lapointe, Godmother: Elisa Ouellette, Pierre St.Germain o.m.i.; married 15 November 1920, Philomene Hamelin. (page 23)

CHARTRAND, Joseph Jean Baptiste: B-22, Joseph Jean Baptiste Chartrand, born 18 November 1899, baptized 19 November 1899, son of Johnny Chartrand and Adelie Rose Piche, Godfather: Jimmy Chartrand, Godmother: Ernestine Briere, Emmanuel Garon priest. (page 35)

CHARTRAND, Joseph Louis Alfred: B-8, Joseph Louis Alfred Chartrand, born 14 July 1901, baptized 20 June 1901, son of Johnny Chartrand and Athalie Piche, Godfather: Albert Legare, Pierre St.Germain o.m.i. (page 38)

CHARTRAND, Joseph Louis Napoleon: B-1, Joseph Louis Napoleon Chartrand, born 2 January 1899, baptized 3 January 1899, son of Johnny Chartrand and Adele Piche, Godfather: Louis Briere, Godmother: Josette Berard, Emmanuel Garon priest. (page 33)

CHARTRAND, Joseph Marc: B-16, Joseph Marc Chartrand, born 14 November 1905, baptized 19 November 1905, son of Johnny Chartrand and Nathalie Rose Piche, Godfather: Marc A. Noel, Godmother: Veronique Chartand, Alphonse Lemieux; married 16 June 1934 Marguerite Short. (page 48)

CHARTRAND, Louis: B-4, Louis Chartrand, born 7 February 1883, baptized 8 February 1883, son of Zacharie Chartrand and Victoire Breland, Godfather: Ambroise Chartrand, Godmother: Francoise Landry, Pierre St.Germain o.m.i. (page 2)

CHARTRAND, Marie: Marie Chartrand, age 4, died 4 July 1899, buried 5 July 1899, Witness: Zacharie Chartrand,

St.Ignace Parish of Willow Bunch, Saskatchewan
1882-1910, Baptisms, Marriages and Burials

Emmanuel Garon priest. (page 138)

CHARTRAND, Marie Elise: B-12, Marie Elise Chartrand, born 31 August 1889, baptized 31 August 1889, daughter of Johny Chartrand and Nathalie Rose Piche, Godfather: Louis Piche, Godmother: Cecile Desmarais, Pierre St.Germain o.m.i. (page 17)

CHARTRAND, Marie Elise and Francois GOSSELIN: M-2, Francois Gosselin, son of Alexandre Gosselin and Marie Champagne, married 12 April 1910, Marie Elise Chartrand, daughter of Zacharie Chartrand and Victoire Breland, Witness: Alexandre Gosselin and Zacharie Chartrand, Alphonse Lemieux priest. (page 116)

CHARTRAND, Marie Elise Victoire: B-10, Marie Elise Victoire Chartrand, born 30 July 1893, baptized 30 July 1893, daughter of Zacharie Chartrand and Victoire Breland, Godfather: Gaspard Beaupre, Godmother: Florestine Piche, Pierre St.Germain o.m.i., married 13 April 1910, Francois Gosselin. (page 23)

CHARTRAND, Marie Elize: Marie Elize Chartrand, age _, died 31 August 1889, buried 1 September 1889, Witness: Alexandre McGillis, Pierre St.Germain priest. (page 137)

CHARTRAND, Marie Eugenie: B-10, Marie Eugenie Chartrand, born 13 March 1908, baptized 16 March 1908, daughter of Jean Chartrand and Athalie Piche, Godfather: Alexandre Rivard, Godmother: Francoise Delorme, Alphonse Lemieux priest. (page 54)

CHARTRAND, Marie Nathalie: B-11, Marie Natalie Chartrand, born 13 May 1900, baptized 13 May 1900, daughter of Zacharie Chartrand and Victoire Breland, Godfather: Alexander McGillis, Godmother: Isabelle Fagnan, Emmanuel Garon priest. (page 36)

CHARTRAND, Marie Priscille: B-18, Marie Priscille Chartrand, born 8 December 1895, baptized 10 December 1895, daughter of Zacharie Chartrand and Victoire Breland, Godfather: Jean Marie Whiteford, Godmother: Genevieve Whiteford, A. Leuret priest. (page 27)

CHARTRAND, Marie Virginie: B-22, Marie Virginie Chartrand, born 15 October 1885, baptized 15 October 1885, daughter of Zacharie Chartrand and Victoire Breland, Godfather: Jean Chartrand, Godmother: Marie Athalie Piche, Pierre St.Germain o.m.i. (page 9)

CHARTRAND, St.Pierre: B-12, St.Pierre Chartrand, born 23 July 1895, baptized 25 July 1895, daughter of Johnny Chartrand and Athalie Rose Piche, Godfather: Joseph Hamelin, Godmother: Isabelle Piche, A. Leuret priest; married 7 February 1922, Marie Rose Short. (page 27)

CHARTRAND, Veronique: B-7, Veronique Chartrand, born 27 June 1887, baptized 2 July 1887, daughter of Johnny Chartrand and Nathalie Rose Piche, Godfather: Gapard Beaupre, Godmother: Florestine Piche, Pierre St.Germain o.m.i. (page 13)

CHARTRAND, Veronique: Veronique Chartrand, wife of Julien Delorme, age 24, buried 9 March 1911, Alphonse Lemieux priest. (page 140)

CHARTRAND, Virginie and Eusebe PERRAS: M-2, Eusebe Pierre Perras, son of Eusebe Perras and Ernestine Page, married 16 April 1907, Virginie Chartrand, daughter of Zacharie Chartrand and Victoire Breland, Witness: Gaspard Beaupre and Narcisse Lacerte, Alphonse Lemieux priest. (page 115)

CHARTRAND, Zacharie: B-2, Zacharie Chartrand, born 26 March 1891, baptized 27 March 1891, son of Zacharie Chartrand and Victoire Breland, Godfather: Louis Dumais, Godmother: Eloiza Caplette, Pierre St.Germain o.m.i.;

married 25 July 1911, Marie Agathe McGillis. (page 19)

CLOUSTRE, Pierre: B-7, Pierre Cloustre, born 6 February 1886, baptized 29 March 1886, son of Jean Cloustre and _, Godfather: Pierre Louis Cloustre, Godmother: Marie Rose Leveille, Pierre St.Germain o.m.i. (page 10)

CONNOR, Georges and Marie Rose MITCHEL: M-1, Georges Connor, married 22 January 1884, Marie Rose Mitchel, Witness: Maxime Carrufel and Napoleon Myette, Pierre St.Germain o.m.i. (page 110)

CONTOIS, Pierre: Pierre Contois, husband of Helene Caplette, age 54, buried, 21 December 1908, Alphonse Lemieux priest. (page 139)

COOK, Caroline: Caroline Cook, wife of Jean Baptiste Lafournaise, age _, died 8 January 1888, buried 9 January 1888, Pierre St.Germain priest. (page 137)

CURRAT, Leon and Maria LAUTIER: M-4, Leon Currat, son of Antoine Currat (Swiss) and Reine _, married 29 October 1906, Maria Lautier, daughter of Raymond Lautier and Francoise Blanche, Witness: Alfred Currat and Virginie Chartrand, Alphonse Lemieux priest. (page 115)

DAUGHTERTY, Mary Kathleen: B-19, Mary Kathleen Daugherty, born 17 May 1885, baptized 12 October 1885, daughter of James Benjamin Daugherty and Elisabeth Dowdell, Godfather: James Ryan, Godmother: Kathleen Daugherty, Pierre St.Germain o.m.i. (page 8)

DAUPHINAIS, Jean: B-3, Jean Dauphinais, born 27 September 1882, baptized 12 November 1882, son of Alexis Dauphinais and Philomene Carrierre, Godfather: Pierre Norn, Godmother: Marguerite Raineault, Pierre St.Germain o.m.i. (page 1)

DAUPHINAIS, Marie Claudina: B-7, Marie Claudina Dauphinais, born 9 February 1883, baptized 10 February 1883, daughter of Casimir Dauphinais and Marie Breland, Godfather: Francois Dauphinais, Godmother: Marie Rose Morin, Pierre St.Germain o.m.i. (page 2)

DAUPHINAIS, Simeon Henri Eugene: B-24, Simeon Henri Eugene Daupinais, born 15 September 1908, baptized 20 September 1908, son of Alphonse Dauphinais and Adelaide Lesperance, Godfather: Simeon Ducharme, Godmother: Marie Lesperance, Alphonse Lemieux priest. (page 55)

DE LAFOREST, Paul Marie Edouard: B-23, Paul Marie Edouard de Laforest, born 16 September 1908, baptized 20 September 1908, son of Edouard de Laforest and Elisa Letourneau, Godfather: Ovila Letourneau, Godmother: Rebecca Letourneau, Alphonse Lemieux priest. (page 55)

DE LA RIVIERE, Madeleine Marie Josephe: B-21, Madeleine Marie Josephe de La Riviere, born 9 August 1908, baptized 23 August 1908, daughter of Xavier de La Riviere and Marguerite de Villele, Godfather: Joseph de La Riviere, Godmother: Madeleine de La Riviere, Alphonse Lemieux priest. (page 55)

DE LA RIVIERE, Marie Anne Charlotte: B-6, Marie Anne Charlotte de La Riviere, born 4 February 1907, baptized 16 February 1907, daughter of Xavier de La Riviere and Marguerite de Villele, Godfather: Charles de Villele, Godmother: Marie Anne Tzeuie, M. Mesnage vic. (page 51)

DEEGAN, Marguerite Elisabeth: B-7, Marguerite Elisabeth Deegan, born 14 November 1882, baptized 6 December 1882, daughter of James Deegan and Marguerite Pelletier, Godfather: Mathias Desjarlais, Godmother: Melanie Pelletier, Pierre St.Germain o.m.i. (page 1)

St.Ignace Parish of Willow Bunch, Saskatchewan
1882-1910, Baptisms, Marriages and Burials

DEGRAND, Joseph: Joseph Degrand, infant of Joseph Degrand, age 6 months, 7 April 1910, Alphonse Lemieux priest. (page 140)

DEGRAND, Joseph Adjutor: B-26, Joseph Adjutor Degrand, born 14 October 1909, baptized 17 October 1909, son of Joseph Degrand and Elisabeth Dandeneau, Godfather: Adjutor Myette, Godmother: Josette Laurte, Alphonse Lemieux priest. (page 59)

DEGRAND, Marie Amelia: B-14, Marie Amelia Degrand, born 18 September 1907, baptized 22 September 1907, daughter of Joseph Degrand and Elisabeth Dandeneau, Godfather: Delphis Wayette, A. Degrand, Alphonse Lemieux priest; married 31 August 1927 Raymond Varseu [?]. (page 52)

DELORME, Ambroise and Philomene PELLETIER: M-4, Ambroise Delorme, married 28 April 1883, Philomene Pelletier, Witness: Joesph Lapointe and Pierre Pelletier, Pierre St.Germain o.m.i. (page 110)

DELORME, Anonyme: Anonyme Delorme, infant of Julien Delorme, age 0, buried, 29 March 1911, Alphonse Lemieux priest. (page 140)

DELORME, Francoise: Francoise Delorme, spouse of Antoine Gosselin, age 58, died 14 June 1899, buried 16 June 1899, Emmanuel Garon priest. (page 138)

DELORME, Joseph Edward: B-9, Joseph Edouard Delorme, born 12 February 1883, baptized 12 February 1883, son of Charles Delorme and Isabelle Piche, Godfather: Gaspard Beaupre, Godmother: Florestine Piche, Pierre St.Germain o.m.i. (page 3)

DESCHAMPS, Caroline: B-21, Caroline Deschamps, born 20 July 1882, baptized 7 May 1883, daughter of Jean Baptiste Deschamps and _, Godfather: Napoleon Turcotte, Godmother: Madeleine Deschamps, Pierre St.Germain o.m.i. (page 4)

DESMARAIS, Alfred and Marguerite HENNERY: M-4, Alfred Desmarais, minor son of Joseph Desmarais and Rosalie St.Denis, married 2 July 1901, Marguerite Hennery, minor daughter of Andre Hennery [Allary] and Josette McGillis, Witness: Alexandre Breiere and Gregoire McGillis, Pierre St.Germain o.m.i. (page 114)

DESMARAIS, Joseph Alfred: B-15, Joseph Alfred Desmarais, born 5 March 1883, baptized 11 March 1883, son of Joseph Desmarais and Roslaie St.Denis, Godfather: Daniel Dumais, Godmother: Elise Ferguson, Pierre St.Germain o.m.i. (page 3)

DONEY, Clemence: B-21, Clemence Donais, born 13 October 1883, baptized 4 July 1886, daughter of Leonide Doney and Marie Angelique Morin, Godfather: David Langer, Godmother: Marie Page, Pierre St.Germain o.m.i. (page 12)

DONEY, Jean Baptiste: B-22, Jean Baptiste Donais [Doney], born 2 November 1885, baptized 4 July 1886, son of Leonide Donais [Doney] and Marie Angelique Morin, Godfather: Joseph Morin, Godmother: Eliza Desjarlais, Pierre St.Germain o.m.i. (page 12)

DOYLE, Mary Ellen: B-3, Mary Ellen Doyle, born January 1896 Moose Jaw, baptized 18 February 1896, daughter of Patrick Doyle and Maggie Spagnton, Godfather: _ Leary, Godmother: Mrs. Green, A. Leuret priest. (page 28)

DOYLE, Patrick: B-17, Patrick Doyle, born 30 March 1897, baptized 10 December 1897, son of Patrick Doyle and Margaret Spangton, Godfather: P. E. Hickey, Godmother: Jane Kergan, Pierre St.Germain o.m.i. (page 31)

DEBRUIL, Louis and Marie LAFOURNAISE: M-3, Louis Dubreuil, adult son of Billy Dubreuil and Marie Malaterre, married 21 May 1900, Marie Lafournaise, minor daughter of Napoleon Lafournaise and Therese McGillis, Witness: Guilluame Klyne and Rev. Pierre St.Germain o.m.i., Emmanuel Garon priest. (page 113)

DURFRESNE, Joseph: Joseph Dufresne, age 68, buried 14 November 1913, Witness: Edmond Lesperance, Alphonse Lemieux priest. (page 141)

DUMAIS, Agnes: Agnes Dumais, age 1, died 4 April 1899, buried 5 April 1899, Witness: Jean Baptiste Dumais, Emmanuel Garon priest. (page 138)

DUMAIS, Anne Marie: B-21, Anne Marie Dumais, born 21 November 1904, baptized 27 November 1904, daughter of Jean Baptiste Dumais and _ Piche, Godfather: Francois Gervais, Godmother: Celina Piche, C. J. Passaplan priest; married 2 June 1922 Emile Short. (page 46)

DUMAIS, Charles: Charles Dumas, died 6 August 1903, buried 16 August 1903, C. J. Passaplan. (page 139)

DUMAIS, Francoise: Francoise Dumais, infant of Louis Dumais, christened and buried 26 Mar 1911, A. Lemieux priest. (page 140)

DUMAIS, Jean Baptiste and Vitaline PICHE: M-2, Jean Baptiste Dumais, son of Charles Dumais and Marie St.Arnaud, married 26 April 1893, Vitaline Piche, daughter of Louis Piche and Cecile Desmarais, Witness: Delphis Short and Louis Dumais, Pierre St.Germain o.m.i. (page 112)

DUMAIS, Joseph Alfred Oscar: B-23, Joseph Alfred (Oscar) Dumais, born 8 October 1902, baptized 10 October 1902, son of Jean Baptiste Dumas and Vitaline Piche, Godfather: Johnny Chartrand, Godmother: Veroniuqe Chartrand, C. J. Passaplan priest. (page 41)

DUMAIS, Joseph Gaspard Oscar: B-20, Joseph Gaspard Oscar Dumais, born 13 September 1906, baptized 17 September 1906, son of Jean Baptiste Dumais and Vitaline Piche, Godfather: Gaspard Beaupre, Godmother: Florestine Piche, Alphonse Lemieux priest; married 3 March 1930 Evelyn Gosselin. (page 50)

DUMAIS, Louis and Ernestine BRIERE: M-3, Louis Dumais, widower of Elisa Caplette, married 3 November 1908, Ernestine Briere, daughter of Louison Briere and Josette Berard, Witness: Gaspard Beaupre and Zacharie Chartrand, Alphonse Lemieux priest. (page 115)

DUMAIS, Marie Adeline: B-4, Marie Adeline Dumais, born 18 February 1894, baptized 19 February 1894, daughter of Jean Baptiste Dumais and Vitaline Piche, Godfather: Zacharie Piche, Godmother: Justine Piche, A. Leuret priest. (page 24)

DUMAIS, Marie Cecile: B-2, Marie Cecile Dumais, born 3 February 1896, baptized 4 February 1896, daughter of Jean Baptiste Dumais and Vitaline Piche, Godfather: Louis Dumais, Godmother: Elise Caplette, A. Leuret priest. (page 28)

DUMAIS, Marie Cecile: Marie Cecile Dumais, age 4, died 25 April 1899, buried 27 April 1899, Witness: Jean Baptiste Dumais, Emmanuel Garon priest. (page 138)

DUMAIS, Marie Philomene: B-4, Marie Philomene Dumais, born 29 March 1900, baptized 29 March 1900, daughter of Baptiste Dumais and Vitaline Piche, Godfather: Joseph Hamelin, Godmother: Philomene Piche, Emmanuel Garon priest. (page 35)

St.Ignace Parish of Willow Bunch, Saskatchewan
1882-1910, Baptisms, Marriages and Burials

DUMAIS, Victoria: B-6, Victoria Dumais, born 29 March 1909, baptized 4 April 1909, daughter of Jean Baptiste Dumais and Vitaline Piche, Godfather: Henri Roy, Godmother: Helene Dumais, Alphonse Lemieux priest; married 26 December 1927 Delphis Rivard. (page 57)

DUMANCEAU, __: Dumanceau, died 6 July 1910, buried 8 July 1910, Alphonse Lemieux priest. (page 140)

DUMOND, Marie Melina: Marie Melina Dumond, infant of Joseph Dumond, age 3 months, buried 9 July 1910, Alphonse Lemieux priest. (page 140)

DUMONT, Eliza: Eliza Dumont, age 10, died 26 April 1900, buried 28 April 1900, Witness: Louis Dumont, Emmanuel Garon priest. (page 138)

DUMONT, Francois and Monique BELLEROSE: M-2, Francois Dumont, son of Vital Dumont and Adelaide Gagnon, married 2 March 1883, Monique Bellerose, daughter of Olivier Bellerose and Catherine Surprenant, Witness: Mathias Sansregret and Louis Dumais, Pierre St.Germain o.m.i. (page 110)

DUMONT, Francois Xavier: Francois Xavier Dumont, age 7, died 26 March 1902, buried 28 March 1902, Witness: Antoine Gosselin, Pierre St.Germain priest. (page 139)

DUMONT, Joseph Patrice Toussaint: B-19, Joseph Patrice Toussaint, Dumont, born 5 October 1899, baptized 5 November 1899, son of Louis Dumont and Philomene Thomas, Godfather: Louis Dumais, Godmother: Elisa Caplette, Emmanuel Garon priest. (page 34)

DUMONT, Louis: Louis Dumont, son of Pierre Dumont, age 12 months, buried 5 March 1906, M. Mesnage priest V. (page 139)

DUMONT, Louis Riel: B-3, Louis Riel Dumont, born 23 February 1905, baptized 26 February 1905, son of Pierre Dumont (deceased) and Athalie McGillis, Godfather: Louis Riel McGillis, Mathilde McGillis, C. J. Passaplan priest. (page 47)

DUMONT, Marie Josephine: B-9, Marie Josephine Dumont, born 22 June 1907, baptized 28 June 1907, son of Joseph Dumont and Marie Adam, Godfather: Antoine Caplette, Godmother: Nathalie Trottier, Alphonse Lemieux priest. (page 52)

DUMONT, Marie Julianne: B-14, Marie Julianne Dumont, born 6 February 1899, baptized 25 September 1899, daughter of Alexis Dumont and Sarah Morin, Godfather: Joseph Botineau (pere), Godmother: Louise Vallie, Emmanuel Garon priest. (page 34)

DUMONT, Marie Philomene: B-9, Marie Philomene Dumont, born 28 August 1901, baptized 15 September 1901, daughter of Joseph Dumont and Josephine Adam, Godfather: Louis Dumont, Godmother: Philomene Roussain, Pierre St.Germain o.m.i. (page 38)

DUMONT, Norbert: B-2, Norbert Dumont, born 22 February 1904, baptized 27 February 1904, son of Joseph Dumont and Josephine Adam, Godfather: Norbert McGillis, Godmother: Pauline McGillis, C. J. Passaplan priest. (page 44)

DUMONT, Patrice: Patrice Dumont, age 1, died 13 May 1901, buried 14 May 1901, Witness: Napoleon Fagnant, Pierre St.Germain priest. (page 139)

DUMONT, Pierre: B-11, Pierre Dumont, born June 1882, baptized 27 December 1882, son of Louis Dumont and

Philomene Thomas, Godfather: Pierre Ledoux, Godmother: Catherine Dumais, Pierre St.Germain o.m.i. (page 2)

DUMONT, Rosalie and Louis THOMAS: M-1, Louis Thomas, son of Bernard Thomas and Lisa St.Denis, married 4 May 1908, Rosalie Dumont, daughter of Louis Dumont and Philomene Roussin, Witness: Tobie McGillis and Pierre Lavallee, Alphonse Lemieux priest. (page 115)

DUMONT, Rosalie: Rosalie Dumont, age 11, died 28 July 1910, buried 30 July 1910, Alphonse Lemieux priest. (page 140)

DUPRENEAULT, Joseph Trever Gaston: B-5, Joseph Trever Gaston Dupreneault, born 3 April 1909, baptized 7 April 1909, son of Joseph Dupreneault and Marie Anne Boucher, Godfather: Romuald Granger, Godmother: Marie Louise _, Alphonse Lemieux priest; married 9 December 1931 Marie Anne Dionne. (page 57)

ESQUAQUEMCANE, Joseph William: B-8, Joseph William Esquaquemcane (Indian), born 1883, baptized 24 March 1886, Parents Indian, Godfather: Joseph Tanner, Godmother: Francois Laronde, Pierre St.Germain o.m.i. (page 10)

FAGNAN, Lucie Guillemine and Jean Baptiste ROY: M-1, Jean Baptiste Roy, married 1 March 1892, Lucie Guillelmine Fagnan, daughter of Jean Baptiste Fagnan and Angelique Ward, Witness: Jean Baptiste Fagnan and Napoleon McGillis, Pierre St.Germain o.m.i. (page 112)

FAGNAN, Marie Rose and Joseph GOSSELIN: M-3, Joseph Gosselin, son of Antoine Gosselin and Francoise Delorme, married 11 May 1892, Marie Rose Fagnan, daughter of Jean Baptiste Fagnan and Angelique Ward, Witness: Alexandre Gosselin and Jean Baptiste Fagnan Jr., Pierre St.Germain o.m.i. (page 112)

FAGNANT, Jean Baptiste: Jean Baptiste Fagnant, age 79, Witness: Pierre Lavallee, buried 3 March 1915, A. Lemieux priest. (page 141)

FAGNANT, Joseph: B-14, Joseph Fagnant, born 26 January 1883, baptized 2 March 1883, son of William Fagnant and Marguerite Denomme, Godfather: Isidore Amyot, Godmother: Rose Denomme, Pierre St.Germain o.m.i. (page 3)

FAGNANT, Marie Angelique: B-16, Marie Angelique Fagnant, born 7 February 1886, baptized 8 March 1886, daughter of Jean Louis Fagnant and Elise Plante, Godfather: Moise Adam, Godmother: Marie Leveille, Pierre St.Germain o.m.i. (page 11)

FOY, Marthe: Marthe Foy, age 40, died 24 May 1908, buried 26 May 1908, Alphonse Lemieux priest. (page 139)

GARIEPY, Marie Madeleine: B-20, Marie Madeleine Gariepy, born 7 September 1885, baptized 9 October 1885, daughter of Bonaparte Gariepy and Catherine Larocque, Godfather: Alexandre Gariepy, Godmother: Mathilde Gariepy, Pierre St.Germain o.m.i. (page 8)

GARIEPY, Rose: B-2, Rose Gariepy, born 18 March 1885, baptized 30 March 1885, daughter of Baptiste Gariepy and Helene Crisse, Godfather: Charles Champagne, Godmother: Elisa Ouellette, Pierre St.Germain o.m.i. (page 6)

GAUDRY, Alfred: B-14, Alfred Gaudry, born 11 September 1895, baptized 15 September 1895, son of Andre Gaudry and Marie Beauchamp, Godfather: Pierre Briere, Godmother: Marie Briere, A. Leuret priest. (page 27)

GAUDRY, Alice: B-27, Alice Gaudry, born 19 November 1909, baptized 21 November 1909, daughter of Jimmy Gaudry and Cecile St.Denis, Godfather: Patrice St.Denis, Godmother: Louise Leveille, Alphonse Lemieux priest. (page 59)

St.Ignace Parish of Willow Bunch, Saskatchewan
1882-1910, Baptisms, Marriages and Burials

GAUDRY, Amable: B-3, Amable Gaudry, born 18 February 1884, baptized 20 February 1884, son of Andre Gaudry and Marie Beauchamp, Godfather: Joseph Charrette, Godmother: Rosalie Colin, Pierre St.Germain o.m.i. (page 6)

GAUDRY, Anne: B-13, Anne Gaudry, born 19 September 1909, baptized 19 September 1909, daughter of Louis Gaudry and Helene [Adeline] Bellegarde, Godfather: Abraham Beauchamp, Godmother: Marie Louise Desjardins, Alphonse Lemieux priest. (page 59)

GAUDRY, Augustin: B-15, Augustin Gaudry, born 16 June 1903, baptized 17 June 1903, son of Moise Gaudry and Florestine Lacerte, Godfather: Andre Gaudry, Godmother: Julie Caplette, C. J. Passaplan priest. (page 43)

GAUDRY, Auxilia: Auxilia Gaudry, died 13 August 1894, buried 15 August 1894, A. Lerch priest. (page 138)

GAUDRY, Damase: B-2, Damase Gaudry, born 17 January 1888, baptized 3 June 1888, son of Andre Gaudry and Marie Beauchamp, Godfather: Octave Gaudry, Godmother: Adelaide Hogue, Pierre St.Germain o.m.i., married, 19 November 1911, Rosalie Gosselin, page 24) (page 15)

GAUDRY, Damase: B-18, Damas Gaudry, born 18 July 1909, baptized 8 August 1909, son of Moise Gaudry and Florestine Lacerte, Godfather: Damase Gaudry, Godmother: Marie Lacerte, Alphonse Lemieux priest. (page 58)

GAUDRY, Ernest: B-6, Ernest Gaudry, born 29 April 1905, baptized 1 May 1905, son of Moise Gaudry and Florestine Lacerte, Godfather: Narcisse Lacerte, Godmother: Seraphine Ouellette, C. J. Passaplan priest; married 29 April 1928 Rose Dumont. (page 47)

GAUDRY, Francois: B-20, Francois Gaudry, born 4 April 1905, baptized 11 November 1905, son of Jimmy Gaudry and Cecile St.Denis, Godfather: Joseph Laplante, Godmother: Josette St.Denis, Alphonse Lemieux priest. (page 48)

GAUDRY, Helene: B-3, Helene Gaudry, born 24 September 1889, baptized 30 April 1890, daughter of Andre Gaudry and Marie Beauchamp, Godfather: Napoleon McGillis, Godmother: Rose McGillis, Pierre St.Germain o.m.i. (page 18)

GAUDRY, Helene: Helene Gaudry, age 7 months, buried 6 May 1890, Witness: Angus McGillis, Pierre St.Germain priest. (page 137)

GAUDRY, Helene [CHARRON dit DUCHARME]: Helene Gaudry, age 84, Witness: A. Gaudry, buried 5 December 1911, Alphonse Lemieux priest. (page 140)

GAUDRY, Jean Bernard: B-4, Jean Bernard Gaudry, born 8 April 1907, baptized 15 April 1907, son of Moise Gaudry and Florestine Lacerte, Godfather: Bernard Langer, Godmother: Marie Beauchamp, Alphonse Lemieux priest; married Toronto 4 March 1935 Margaret Dunn. (page 50)

GAUDYR, Jean Marie: B-1, Jean Marie Gaudry, born 31 January 1892, baptized 31 January 1892, son of Andre Gaudry and Marie Beauchamp, Godfather: Jean Marie McGillis, Godmother: Isabelle Fagnan; P. St.Germain o.m.i. (page 21)

GAUDRY, Jean Marie: Jean Marie Gaudry, age 4 months, died 1 June 1892, buried 3 June 1892, Witness: Moise Gaudry, Pierre St.Germain priest. (page 138)

GAUDRY, Joseph Albert: B-3, Joseph Albert Gaudry, born 7 February 1893, baptized 9 February 1893, son of Andre Gaudry and Marie Beauchamp, Godfather: Alexandre McGillis, Godmother: Marie Jeannotte, Pierre

St.Ignace Parish of Willow Bunch, Saskatchewan
1882-1910, Baptisms, Marriages and Burials

St.Germain o.m.i. (page 22)

GAUDRY, Joseph Felix Alexandre: B-9, Joseph Felix Alexandre Gaudry, born 11 May 1899, baptized 14 May 1899, son of Andre Gaudry and Marie Beauchamp, Godfather: Bernard Beauchamp, Godmother: Emma Lacerte, Emmanuel Garon priest. (page 33)

GAUDRY, Joseph Janivier: B-1, Joseph Janvier Gaudry, born 1 January 1908, baptized 2 January 1908, son of Joseph Gaudry and Marie Chartrand, Godfather: Bernard Langer, Godmother: Marie Gaudry, Alphonse Lemieux priest. (page 53)

GAUDRY, Louis: B-2, Louis Gaudry, baptized 22 October 1882, son of Andre Gaudry and Marie Beauchamp, Godfather: Joseph Lapointe, Godmother: Florestine Piche, Pierre St.Germain o.m.i. (page 1)

GAUDRY, Louis: B-25, Louis Gaudry, born 14 December 1903, baptized 19 December 1903, son of Jimmy Gaudry and Cecile St.Denis, Godfather: Louis Laplante, Godmother: Virginie Fleury, C. J. Passaplan priest. (page 44)

GAUDRY, Louis and Adeline BELLEGARDE: M-3, Louis Gaudry, minor son of Andre Gaudry and Marie Beauchamp, married 4 June 1901, Adeline Bellegarde, minor daughter of Pierre Bellegarde and Marie Fidler, Witness: Moise Gaudry and Bernard Langer, Pierre St.Germain o.m.i. (page 114)

GAUDRY, Louis: Louis Gaudry, died 13 March 1904, buried 2 April 1904, Witness: Jimmy Gaudry, C. J. Passaplan. (page 139)

GAUDRY, Louis Simeon: B-3, Louis Simeon Gaudry, born 11 February 1886, baptized 15 February 1886, son of Andre Gaudry and Marie Beauchamp, Godfather: Louis Legare, Godmother: Emerise Lafournaise, Pierre St.Germain o.m.i. (page 10)

GAUDRY, Marie GAUDRY: B-12, Marie Gaudry, born 24 June 1904, baptized 26 June 1904, daughter of Joseph Gaudry and Marie Helene Chartrand, Godfather: Ambroise Chartrand, Godmother: Helene Briere, C. J. Passaplan priest. (page 45)

GAUDRY, Marie and Bernard LANGER: M-1, Bernard Langer, adult son of David Langer and Marie Page, married 30 January 1900, Marie Gaudry, adult daughter of Andre Gaudry and Marie Beauchamp, Witness: Andre Gaudry and Treffle Bonneau, Emmanuel Garon priest. (page 113)

GAUDRY, Marie Antala: B-23, Marie Antala Gaudry, born 10 December 1906, baptized 16 December 1906, daughter of Louis Gaudry and Adeline Bellegarde, Godfather: Damase Gaudry, Godmother: Josette Lacerte, Alphonse Lemieux priest. (page 51)

GAUDRY, Marie Auxilia: B-3, Marie Auxilia Gaudry, 5 February 1894, 6 February 1894, daughter of Andre Gaudry and Marie Beauchamp, Godfather: Bernard Beauchamp, Godmother: Marie Desjardins, A. Leuret priest. (page 24)

GAUDRY, Marie Helene: B-9, Marie Helene Gaudry, born 11 April 1906, baptized 13 April 1906, daughter of Joseph Gaudry and Marie Helene Chartrand, Godfather: Andre Gaudry, Godmother: Marie Beauchamp, Alphonse Lemieux priest; married Shell River 21 August 1932 Charles Bonneau. (page 49)

GAUDRY, Marie Malvina: B-22, Marie Malvina Gaudry, born 11 December 1900, baptized 12 December 1900, daughter of Andre Gaudry and Marie Beauchamp, Godfather: Moise Gaudry, Godmother: Marie Gosselin, Pierre St.Germain o.m.i. (page 37)

GAUDRY, Marie Malvina: Malvina Gaudry, age 9 months, died 4 September 1901, buried 5 September 1901, Witness: Andre Gaudry, Pierre St.Germain priest. (page 139)

GAUDRY, Marie Rosalie: B-15, Marie Rosalie Gaudry, born 4 October 1907, baptized 6 October 1907, daughter of Jimmy Gaudry and Cecile St.Denis, Godfather: Andre Gaudry, Godmother: Marie Beauchamp, Alphonse Lemieux priest. (Page 52)

GAUDRY, Marie Rose: B-7, Marie Rose Gaudry, born 14 May 1901, baptized 15 May 1901, daughter of Joseph Gaudry and Helene Chartrand, Godfather: Zacharie Chartrand, Godmother: Francoise Landry, Pierre St.Germain o.m.i. (page 38)

GAUDRY, Moise and Florestine LACERTE: M-2, Moise Gaudry, adult son of Andre Gaudry and Marie Beauchamp, married 3 June 1902, Florestine Lacerte, minor daughter of Narcisse Lacerte and Julie Caplette, Witness: _, C. Passaplan priest. (page 114)

GAUDRY, Octave: B-9, Octave Gaudry, born 13 November 1890, baptized 21 December 1890, son of Octave Gaudry and Adelaide Roque, Godfather: Bernard Beauchamp, Godmother: Philomene McGillis, Pierre St.Germain o.m.i., married 20 November 1917, Eva Balaux. (page 18)

GAUDRY, Philomene: Philomene Gaudry, died 8 June 1900, buried 10 June 1900, Witness: Gregoire McGillis, Pierre St.Germain priest. (page 138)

GAUDRY, Pierre: B-4, Pierre Gaudry, born 15 February 1891, baptized 13 April 1891, son of Andre Gaudry and Marie Beauchamp, Godfather: Bernard Beauchamp, Godmother: Marie Gaudry, Pierre St.Germain o.m.i. (page 19)

GAUDRY, Pierre: Pierre Gaudry, age 1, died 1 February 1892, buried 2 February 1892, Witness: Bernard Beauchamp, Pierre St.Germain priest. (page 138)

GAVIN, Patrick James: B-13, Patrick James Gavin, born 15 July 1885, baptized 18 August 1885, son of Edward Gavin and Marguerite Mooney, Godfather: Thomas Murray, Godmother: Horora Kaughton, Pierre St.Germain o.m.i. (page 8)

GEORGES, Albert Alexis Joseph: B-25, Albert Alexis Joseph Georges, born 21 August 1909, baptized 5 October 1909, son of Leon Georges and Christine Auger, Godfather: Constantin Auger, Godmother: Felicie Auger, Alphonse Lemieux priest; married Santa Monica, 31 December 1929, Josephine Rudy [?]. (page 59)

GEORGES, Leon Alexis and Marie Honorine Christine AUGER: M-4, Leon Alexis Georges, son of Alexis Georges and Jeanne Marie Letriquet, married Marie Honorine Christine Auger, daughter of Constantin Auger and Marie Felice _, Witness: Treffle Bonneau, D. A. Godin, Alphonse Lemieux priest. (page 116)

GIRARD, Hector Olivier: B-11, Hector Olivier Girard, born 8 June 1895, baptized 30 June 1895, son of Henri Girard and Victoria Bonneau, Godfather: Julien Godart, Godmother: Albina Bonneau, A. Leuret priest. (page 27)

GIRARD, Marie Robertine: B-6, Marie Robertine Girard, born 20 April 1894, baptized 24 April 1894, daughter of Henri Girard and Victoire Bonneau, Godfather: Pascal Bonneau, Godmother: Celina Mission, A. Leuret priest. (page 24)

GIRARD, Marie Victoire Virginie: B-5, Marie Victoire Virginie Girard, born 26 November 1896, baptized 9 March 1897, daughter of Henri Girard and Victoire Bonneau, Godfather: Pascal Bonneau, Godmother: Virginie

St.Ignace Parish of Willow Bunch, Saskatchewan
1882-1910, Baptisms, Marriages and Burials

Bellehumeur, Pierre St.Germain o.m.i. (page 30)

GIRARD, Olivier: Olivier Girard, age 5 months, died 31 December 1898, buried 20 February 1898, Witness: Henri Girard, Emmanuel Garon priest. (page 138)

GOSSELIN, Albert: B-5, Albert Gosselin, born 2 May 1907, baptized 7 May 1907, son of Joseph Gaudry and Marie Rose Fagnan, Godfather: Jean Baptiste Fagnan, Godmother: Angelique Fagnan, Alphonse Lemieux priest. (page 51)

GOSSELIN, Alexandre: B-4, Alexandre Gosselin, born 9 March 1895, baptized 10 March 1895, son of Alexandre Gosselin Jr. and Amelie Briere, Godfather: Alexandre Gosselin Sr., Godmother: Francoise Delorme, A. Leuret priest. (page 26)

GOSSELIN, Alexandre and Clemence BRIERE: M-1, Alexandre Gosselin, son of Alexandre Gosselin and Marie Champagne, married 3 January 1887, Clemence Briere, daughter of Louis Briere and Joseph Berard, Witness: Pierre Briere and Francois Lafournaise, Pierre St.Germain o.m.i. (page 111)

GOSSELIN, Alexandre and Emelie BRIERE: M-3, Alexandre Gosselin, son of Antonie Gosselin and Francoise Delorme, married 1 May 1893, Emilie Briere, daughter of Louis Briere and Josette Berard, Witness: Theophile McGillis and Pierre Briere, Pierre St.Germain o.m.i. (page 112)

GOSSELIN, Alexandre and Marie Therese BRIERE
M-1, Alexandre Gosselin, son of Alexandre Gosselin and Marie Champagne, married 8 August 1903, Marie Therese Briere, C. J. Passaplan priest. (page 114)

GOSSELIN, Alphee: Alphee Gosselin, age _, died 7 February 1891, buried 9 February 1891, Witness: Paul Caplette, Pierre St.Germain priest. (page 137)

GOSSELIN, Anonyme: Anonyme Gosselin, infant of Patrice Gosselin, age 0 days, buried 13 Jan 1911, Lemieux priest. (page 140)

GOSSELIN, Antoine: Antoine Gosselin, age 80, buried 27 July 1912, Alphonse Lemieux priest. (page 140)

GOSSELIN, Caroline: B-5, Caroline Gosslin, born 7 February 1902, baptized 22 February 1902, daughter of Joseph Gosselin and Marie Rose Fagnan, Godfather: Delphis Short, Godmother: Rosalie Gosselin, Pierre St.Germain o.m.i. (page 40)

GOSSELIN, Clemence: B-6, Clemence Gosselin, born 3 March 1906, baptized 6 March 1906, daughter of Alexandre Gosselin and Emilie Briere, Godfather: Zacharie Piche, Godmother: Celina Briere, M. Mesnage vic.; married 11 February 1929 Louis Clement Lacerte. (page 49)

GOSSELIN, Clemence: Clemence Gosselin, age 30, died 6 September 1902, buried 8 September 1902, Witness: Louison Brueyer, C. J. Passaplan. (page 139)

GOSSELIN, Elise: Elise Gosselin, wife of Francois Caplette, age 34, died 24 December 1907, buried 25 December 1907, Alphonse Lemieux priest. (page 139)

GOSSELIN, Emile: B-10, Emelie [Emile] Gosselin, baptized 15 July 1897, born 15 July 1897, child of Joseph Gosselin and Marie Rose Fagnan, Godfather: Antoine Gosselin, Godmother: Francoise Delorme, Pierre St.Germain o.m.i. (page 30) [See 1901 and 1916 Canadian Census]

St.Ignace Parish of Willow Bunch, Saskatchewan
1882-1910, Baptisms, Marriages and Burials

GOSSELIN, Emerence Lucie: B-15, Emerence Lucie Gosselin, born 13 November 1887, baptized 14 November 1887, daughter of Alexandre Gosselin and Marie Champagne, Godfather: Alexandre Gosselin, Godmother: Clemence Briere, Pierre St.Gemain o.m.i.; married 12 April 1910, Louis Lapointe. (page 14)

GOSSELIN, Emmanuel and Caroline HAGGEYT: M-2, Emmanuel Gosselin, son of Alexandre Gosselin and Marie Champagne, married 30 October 1905, Caroline Haggeyt, daughter of Louis Haggeyt and Marie Roy, Witness: Louis Roy and Alexandre Gosselin, Alphonse Lemieux priest. (page 114)

GOSSELIN, Francois and Marie Elise CHARTRAND: M-2, Francois Gosselin, son of Alexandre Gosselin and Marie Champagne, married 12 April 1910, Marie Elise Chartrand, daughter of Zacharie Chartrand and Victoire Breland, Witness: Alexandre Gosselin and Zacharie Chartrand, Alphonse Lemieux priest. (page 116)

GOSSELIN, Georges Alfred: B-3, Georges Alfred Gosslin, born 24 January 1906, baptized 31 January 1906, son of parents unknown, Godfather: Joseph Gosselin, Godmother: Francoise Delorme, Alphonse Lemieux priest. (page 49)

GOSSELIN, Helene and Gregoire Alfred MCGILLIS: M-4, Gregoire Alfred McGillis, adult son of Alexandre McGillis and Marie Jeannotte, married 31 October 1900, Helene Gosselin, minor daughter of Alexandre Gosselin and Marie Champagne, Witness: Jean Marie McGillis and Theophile McGillis, Pierre St.Germain o.m.i. (page 113)

GOSSELIN, Jean Israel: B-3, Jean Israel Gosselin, born 10 February 1907, baptized 11 February 1907, son of Emmanuel Gosselin and Caroline Haggeyt, Godfather: Jean Briere, Godmother: Josette Berard, Alphonse Lemieux priest. (page 51)

GOSSELIN, Jean Louis and Marie LACERTE: M-1, Jean Louis Gosselin, son of Alexandre Gosselin and Marie Champagne, married 10 January 1905, Marie Lacerte, daughter of Narcisse Lacerte and Julie Caplette, Witness: Narcisse Lacerte and Raymond Gosselin, C. J. Passaplan priest. (page 114)

GOSSELIN, Joseph: Joseph Gosselin, age 0, buried 23 January 1906, Witness: Joseph Gosselin, Alphonse Lemieux, priest. (page 139)

GOSSELIN, Joseph and Marie Rose FAGNAN: M-3, Joseph Gosselin, son of Antoine Gosselin and Francoise Delorme, married 11 May 1892, Marie Rose Fagnan, daughter of Jean Baptiste Fagnan and Angelique Ward, Witness: Alexandre Gosselin and Jean Baptiste Fagnan Jr., Pierre St.Germain o.m.i. (page 112)

GOSSELIN, Joseph Albert: B-2, Joseph Albert Gosselin, born 13 January 1908, baptized 17 January 1908, son of Patrice Gosselin and Justine Gardepie, Godfather: Francois Gosselin, Godmother: Emerence Gosselin, Alphonse Lemieux priest. (page 53)

GOSSELIN, Joseph Patrice: B-11, Joseph Patrice Gosselin, born 15 March 1908, baptized 17 March 1908, son of Alexandre Gosselin and Emilie Briere, Godfather: Alphonse Lemieux priest, Godmother: Ernestine Briere, Alphonse Lemieux priest. (page 54)

GOSSELIN, Josette: B-16, Josette Gosselin, born 8 October 1891, baptized 11 October 1891, daughter of Antoine Gosselin and Helene Piche, Godfather: Alexandre Gosselin, Godmother: Marie Gosselin, Pierre St.Germain o.m.i., married 24 February 1914, Joseph Ledoux. (page 20)

GOSSELIN, Josette and Theophile MCGILLIS: M-1, Theophile McGillis, married 29 April 1890, Josette Gosselin, Witness: Antoine Gosselin and Alexandre McGillis, Pierre St.Germain o.m.i. (page 111)

GOSSELIN, Louis: B-2, Louis Gosselin, born 17 January 1907, baptized 21 January 1907, Jean Louis Gosselin and

Maria Lacerte, Godfather: Francois Gosselin, Godmother: Emerence Gosselin, Alphonse Lemieux priest. (page 51)

GOSSELIN, Louis Alfred: B-1, Louis Alfred Gosselin, born 4 February 1897, baptized 3 March 1897, son of Alexandre Gosselin and Emelie Briere, Godfather: Louis Briere, Godmother: Josette Berard, Pierre St.Germain o.m.i.; married 27 June 1929, Marie Helene Riviere. (page 30)

GOSSELIN, Louis Alfred: B-19, Louis Alfred Gosselin, born 26 December 1905, baptized 27 December 1905, son of Jean Louis Gosselin and Marie Lacerte, Godfather: Alexandre Gosselin, Godmother: Marie Therese Briere, Alphonse Lemieux priest. (page 48)

GOSSELIN, Louis Frederic: B-8, Louis Frederic Gosselin, born 26 November 1898, baptized 27 November 1898, Alexandre Gosselin and Emelie Briere, Godfather: Alexandre Rivard, Godmother: Francoise Delorme, Emmanuel Garon priest. (page 32)

GOSSELIN, Louis Joseph: B-20, Louis Joseph Gosselin, born 14 September 1902, baptized 15 September 1902, son of Alexandre Gosselin and Amelie Briere, Godfather: Antoine Gosselin, Godmother: Helen Piche, C J. Passaplan priest. (page 41)

GOSSELIN, Magloire: B-1, Magloire Gosselin, born 6 January 1890, baptized 6 January 1890, son of Antoine Gosselin Jr. and Helene Piche, Godfather: Antoine Gosselin Sr., Godmother: Rosalie Gosselin, Pierre St.Germain o.m.i.; married 9 January 1918, Josephine Boxeur. (page 18)

GOSSELIN, Marie and Bernard THOMAS: M-2, Bernard Thomas, son of Joseph Thomas and Marie Adele _, married 15 May 1906, Marie Gosselin, daughter of Antoine Gosselin and Francoise Delorme, Witness: Louis Dumont and Francois Lafournaise, M. Mesnage priest. (page 115)

GOSSELIN, Marie and Clement LACERTE: M-3, Clement Lacerte, widower of Eleonore Ouellette, son of Narcisse Lacerte and Julie Caplette, married 19 March 1906, Marie Gosselin, daughter of Antoine Gosselin and Helene Piche, Witness: Narcisse Lacerte and Octave Gosselin, Alphonse Lemieux priest. (page 115)

GOSSELIN, Marie Emma: B-29, Marie Emma Gosselin, born 27 November 1909, baptized 5 December 1909, daughter of Raymond Gosselin and Emma Lacerte, Godfather: Antoine Gosselin, Godmother: Josette Lacerte, Alphonse Lemiuex priest; married Frederick Smallwood Thorndike, 30 December 1952, Toronto. (page 59)

GOSSELIN, Marie Genevieve: B-10, Marie Genevieve Gosselin, born 7 June 1895, baptized 9 June 1895, daughter of Joseph Gosselin and Marie Rose Fagnan, Godfather: Napoleon Fagnan, Godmother: Philomene Fagnant, A. Leuret priest; married, 29 January 1918, Louis Morin. (page 26)

GOSSELIN, Marie Helene: B-6, Marie Helene Gosselin, born 18 May 1898, baptized 30 October 1898, daughter of Antoine Gosselin and Helene Piche, Godfather: Louis Dumais, Godmother: Elisa Caplette, Emmanuel Garon priest. (page 32)

GOSSELIN, Marie Jules: B-21, Marie Jules Gosselin, born 18 April 1899, born 19 November 1899, child of Joseph Gosselin and Marie Rose Fagnan, Godfather: Jean Baptiste Roy, Godmother: Wilhelmina Fagnan, Emmanuel Garon priest. (page 35)

GOSSELIN, Marie Rose Adele: B-18, Marie Rose Adele Gosselin, born 28 October 1900, baptized 29 October 1900, daughter of Alexandre Gossellin and Emelie Briere, Godfather: Alexandre Briere, Godmother: Marie Therese Briere, Pierre St.Germain o.m.i.; married 25 April 1922, Alfred Botineau. (page 37)

GOSSELIN, Marie Stella: B-7, Marie Stella Gosselin, born 27 February 1908, baptized 28 February 1908, daughter of Raymond Gosselin and Emma Lacerte, Godfather: Narcisse Lacerte, Godmother: Seraphine Ouellette, Alphonse Lemieux priest; married 8 January 1930 Jacques [..]. (page 54)

GOSSELIN, Octave: B-8, Octave Gosselin, born 24 April 1909, baptized 2 May 1909, son of Jean Louis Gosselin and Maria Lacerte, Godfather: Clement Lacerte, Godmother: Julie Caplette, Alphonse Lemieux priest. (page 57)

GOSSELIN, Philomene and Napoleon HAMELIN: M-1, Napoleon Hamelin, son of Joseph Hamelin and Philomene Piche, married 22 January 1906, Philomene Gosselin, daughter of Antoine Gosselin and Francoise Delorme, Witness: Albert Sauvier and Albert Legare, Alphonse Lemieux priest. (page 115)

GOSSELIN, Pierre: B-5, Pierre Gosselin, born 23 February 1893, baptized 25 February 1893, son of Antoine Gosselin and Helene Piche, Godfather: Delphis Short, Godmother: Vitaline Piche, Pierre St.Germain o.m.i. (page 22)

GOSSELIN, Raymond and Emma LACERTE: M-1, Raymond Gosselin, son of Antoine Gosselin and Francoise Delorme, married 22 January 1907, Emma Lacerte, daughter of Narcisse Lacerte and Seraphine Ouellette, Witness: Antoine Gosselin and Narcisse Lacerte, Alphonse Lemeiux priest. (page 115)

GOSSELIN, Rosalie: B-1, Rosalie Gosselin, born 2 February 1894, baptized 3 February 1894, daughter of Alexandre Gosselin and Amelie Briere, Godfather: Pierre Briere, Godmother: Marie Briere, A. Leuret priest; married 19 March 1911, Damase Gaudry. (page 24)

GOSSELIN, Rosalie and Delphis SHORT: M-1, Delphis Short, son of Joseph Short and Marguerite Houle, married 24 April 1894, Rosalie Gosselin, daughter of Antoine Gosselin and Francoise Delorme, Witness: Joseph Lapointe and Jean Louis Legare, Pierre St.Germain o.m.i., Albert Leuret priest. (page 112)

GOSSELIN, Sarah and Louis LAROCQUE: M-1, Louis Larocque, son of Louis Larocque and Suzanne Ledoux, married 16 February 1886, Sarah Gosselin, daughter of Alexandre Gosselin and Marie Champagne, Witness: Joseph Lapointe and Bernard Hamelin, Pierre St.Germain o.m.i. (page 111)

GOSSELIN, Scholastique: B-2, Scholastique Gosselin, born 9 February 1886, baptized 10 February 1886, daughter of Antoine Gosselin and Helene Piche, Godfather: Joseph Gosselin, Godmother: Cecile Desmarais, Pierre St.Germain, married Jean Riviere. (page 10)

GOSSELIN, Scholastique and Jean RIVIERE: M-1, Jean Riviere, son of Jean Marie Riviere and Marie Leunard (of France), married 9 February 1909, Scholastique Gosselin, daughter of Antoine Gosselin and Helene Piche, Witness: Alexandre Rivard and Antoine Gosselin, Alphonse Lemieux priest. (page 116)

GOSSELIN, Veronique: B-12, Veronique Gosselin, born 5 October 1894, baptized 7 October 1894, daughter of Antoine Gosselin and Helene Piche, Godfather: Raymond Gosselin, Godmother: Josette Gosselin, Alb. Leuret priest. (page 25)

GOSSELIN, Virginie: Virginie Gosselin, age 7 days, buried 2 January 1889, Witness: Louis Piche, Pierre St.Germain priest. (page 137)

GOSSELIN, Virginie: Virginie Gosselin, age 16, died 22 February 1897, buried 3 March 1897, Witness: Louis Dumais, Pierre St.Germain priest. (page 138)

GOSSELIN, Virginie: B-7, Virginie Gosselin, born 25 March 1904, baptized 20 April 1904, daughter of Alexandre

Gosselin and Emilie Briere, Godfather: Joseph Gosselin, Godmother: Marie Rose Fagnan, C. J. Passaplan priest. (page 45)

GOSSELIN, Virginie Vitaline: B-5, Virginie Vitaline Gosselin, born 19 December 1888, baptized 25 December 1888, daughter of Antoine Gosselin and Helene Piche, Godfather: Zacharie Chartrand, Godmother: Victoire Breland, Pierre St.Germain o.m.i. (page 15)

GRANGER, Marie Louise and Philippe MONDOR: M-5, Philippe Mondor, son of Elie Mondor and Erminie Barrette, married 26 October 1909, Marie Louise Granger, daughter of Jean Louis Granger and Louise Legare, Witness: Conrad Legare and Romuald Granger, Alphonse Lemieux priest. (page 116)

HAGGEYT, Caroline and Emmanuel GOSSELIN: M-2, Emmanuel Gosselin, son of Alexandre Gosselin and Marie Champagne, married 30 October 1905, Caroline Haggeyt, daughter of Louis Haggeyt and Marie Roy, Witness: Louis Roy and Alexandre Gosselin, Alphonse Lemieux priest. (page 114)

HAGGE&T, Henriette Jeanne: B-6, Henriette Jeanne Haggeyt, born 28 August 1896, baptized 17 April 1897, daughter of Louis Haggeyt and Marie Roy, Godfather: Louis Dumais, Godmother: Louise Anne Klyne, Pierre St.Germain o.m.i.; married 6 February 1926, Albert Brown. (page 30)

HAGGEYT, Isaac: B-15, Isaac Haggeyt, born 1 June 1900, baptized 24 June 1900, son of Louis Haggeyt and Marie Roy, Godfather: Louis Joseph Haggeyt, Godmother: Josette _, Pierre St.Germain o.m.i. (page 36)

HAGGEYT, Isaac: Isaac Haggeyt, age 11 months, died 22 April 1901, buried 24 April 1901, Witness: Louis Haggeyt, Pierre St.Germain priest. (page 139)

HAGGEYT, Jules: B-3, Jules Haggeyt, born 23 October 1891, baptized 18 April 1892, son of Louis Haggeyt and Marie Roy, Godfather: Louis Roy, Godmother: Marguerite Sauve, Pierre St.Germain o.m.i. (page 21)

HAGGEYT, Marie Marguerite: B-16, Marie Marguerite Haggeyt, born 9 August 1903, baptized 10 August 1903, son of Louis Haggeyt and Marie Roy, Godfather: Louis Roy, Godmother: Marguerite Sauve, C. J. Passaplan priest. (page 43)

HAGGEYT, Marie Suzanne: B-5, Marie Suzanne Haggeyt, born 21 February 1894, baptized 23 February 1894, daughter of Louis Haggeyt and Marie Roy, Godfather: Louis Laplante, Godmother: Eleonore Ouellette, A. Leret priest; married 9 February 1918, Delphis Myette. (page 24)

HAMELIN, Bernard and Marie BRIERE: M-2, Bernard Hamelin, son of Moise Hamelin and Isabelle Wichcoupe, married 1 February 1887, Marie Briere, daughter of Louis Briere and Josette Berard, Witness: Louis Piche and Louis Briere, Pierre St.Germain o.m.i. (page 111)

HAMELIN, Bernard: Bernard Hamelin, spouse of Marie Bruyere, age 32, died 6 April 1894, buried 7 April 1894, A. Lerch priest. (page 138)

HAMELIN, Emilie: B-5, Emilie Hamelin, born 2 January 1887, baptized 9 June 1887, daughter of Jonas Hamelin and _ Patenaude, Godfather: Andre Emery, Godmother: Josette Hamelin, Pierre St.Germain o.m.i. (page 13)

HAMELIN, Josephine: B-7, Josephine Hamelin, born 22 March 1893, baptized 24 March 1893, Bernard Hamelin and Marie Briere, Godfather: Pierre Briere, Godmother: Emelie Briere, Pierre St.Germain o.m.i. (page 22)

HAMELINE, Josephine and Adelard PAQUIN: M-5, Adelard Paquin, son of Louis Paquin and Helene Gaudry, married 17 November 1908, Josephine Hamelin, daughter of Bernard Hamelin and Marie Briere, Witness: Louis Paquin and Pierre Briere, Alphonse Lemieux priest. (page 116)

HAMELIN, Leonide: B-1, Leonide Hamelin, born 13 January 1883, baptized 16 January 1883, son of Salomon Hamelin and Celina Malaterre, Godfather: Jean Baptiste Langer, Godmother: Justine Malaterre, Pierre St.Germain o.m.i. (page 2)

HAMELIN, Louise: B-5, Louise Hamelin, born 18 September 1882, baptized 5 December 1882, daughter of Napoleon Hamelin and Eleonore Hamelin, Godfather: Leon Hamelin, Godmother: Angele Hamelin, Pierre St.Germain o.m.i. (page 1)

HAMELIN, Marie Emelie: B-18, Marie Emelie Hamelin, born 17 December 1887, baptized 19 December 1887, daughter of Bernard Hamelin and Marie Briere, Godfather: Louis Briere, Godmother: Josephte Berard, Pierre St.Germain o.m.i. (page 14)

HAMELIN, Marie Emilie: Marie Emilie Hamelin, age 4, died 13 January 1892, buried 14 January 1892, Witness: Napoleon McGillis, Pierre St.Germain priest. (page 137)

HAMELIN, Marie Madeleine: B-1, Marie Madeleine Hamelin, born 10 January 1907, baptized 13 January 1907, daughter of Napoleon Hamelin and Philomene Gosselin, Godfather: Joseph Hamelin, Godmother: Philomene Piche, Alphonse Lemieux priest. (page 51)

HAMELIN, Marie Therese: B-15, Marie Therese Hamelin, born 25 September 1889, baptized 26 September 1889, daughter of Bernard Hamelin and Marie Briere, Godfather: Joseph Hamelin, Godmother: Philomene Piche, Pierre St.Germain o.m.i.; married 10 August 1915, Rodolphe Legare, (page 17)

HAMELIN, Moise: B-20, Moise Hamelin, born 24 December 1891, baptized 25 December 1891, son of Bernard Hamelin and Marie Briere, Godfather: Andre Gaudry, Godmother: Isabelle Fagnan, Pierre St.Germain o.m.i. (page 20)

HAMELIN, Moise: Moise Hamelin, age 14 [months?], died 27 January 1892, buried 28 January 1892, Witness: Louison Bruyere, Pierre St.Germain priest. (page 137)

HAMELIN, Napoleon and Philomene GOSSELIN: M-1, Napoleon Hamelin, son of Joseph Hamelin and Philomene Piche, married 22 January 1906, Philomene Gosselin, daughter of Antoine Gosselin and Francoise Delorme, Witness: Albert Sauvier and Albert Legare, Alphonse Lemieux priest. (page 115)

HAMELIN, Napoleon Joseph: B-23, Napoleon Joseph Hamelin, born 8 May 1883, baptized 9 September 1883, son of Joseph Hamelin and Philomene Piche, Godfather: Francois Desmarais, Godmother: Cecile Desmarais, Pierre St.Germain o.m.i. (page 4)

HARTMAN, Marie Rose: B-20, Marie Rose Hartman, born 10 November 1899, baptized 16 November 1899, son of Benedict Hartman and Rosine Rocheblave, Godfather: Jean Baptiste Fagnan, Godmother: Theresa Rocheblave, Emmanuel Garon priest. (page 34)

HENNERY, Clara Anne: B-9, Clara Anne Hennery, born 8 July 1884, baptized 24 June 1885, daughter of Patrick Hennery and Marguerite Sinclair, Godfather: Cullen Sinclair, Godmother: Marie Rose Tanner, Pierre St.Germain o.m.i. (page 7)

HENNERY, Marguerite and Alfred DESMARAIS: M-4, Alfred Desmarais, minor son of Joseph Desmarais and

St.Ignace Parish of Willow Bunch, Saskatchewan
1882-1910, Baptisms, Marriages and Burials

Rosalie St.Denis, married 2 July 1901, Marguerite Hennery, minor daughter of Andre Hennery [Allary] and Josette McGillis, Witness: Alexandre Breiere and Gregoire McGillis, Pierre St.Germain o.m.i. (page 114)

HIMBEAULT, Joseph Florian Arthur: B-10, Joseph Florian Arthur Himbeault, born 19 June 1907, baptized 14 July 1907, son of Ulric Himbeault and Sarah Boutin, Godfather: Urbain Audette, Godmother: Adeline Boutin, Alphonse Lemieux priest; married Detroit 25 April 1942 Madeleine Dumery. (page 52)

HOULE, Alfred: B-18, Alfred Old [Houle], born 23 August 1902, baptized 8 September 1902, son of Louison Old [Houle] and Marie Amyot, Godfather: Francois Lafournaise, Godmother: Caroline Klyne, C. J. Passaplan priest. (page 41)

HOULE, Louis and Marie AMYOTTE: M-6, Louis Houle, son of Louis Houle and Marguerite Ross, married 2 September 1883, Marie Amyotte, son of Louis Amyotte and Celina Grandbois [Beriault], Witness: Joseph Short and Zacharie Poitras, Pierre St.Germain o.m.i. (page 110)

HOULE, Marguerite: Marguerite Houle, age _, died 26 August 1885, buried 28 August 1885, Witness: Isidore Ouellette, Pierre St.Germain priest. (page 137)

HOULE, Nancy: B-4, Nancy Houle, born 2 September 1895, baptized 12 March 1896, daughter of Louison Houle and Marie Amyot, A. Leuret priest. (page 28)

HOULE, Seraphine RAINVILLE [HOULE]: Seraphine Rainville, age 58, buried 21 February 1906, M. Mesnage priest V. (page 139)

HOULE, Seraphine: Seraphine Houle, wife of Joseph Rainville, died 17 February 1906, buried 19 February 1906, Alphonse Lemieux priest. (page 139)

HOULE, William: William Houle, age 18 months, died 23 February 1889, buried 26 October 1889, Witness: Louis Houle, Pierre St.Germain priest. (page 137)

JEANOTTE, Marie: Marie Jeannotte, wife of Alexandre McGillis, age 56, buried 5 February 1906, Alphonse Lemieux priest. (page 139)

JEROME, Joseph: Joseph Jerome, age 88, buried 13 July 1917, Alphonse Lemieux priest. (page 142)

KENNEDY, Joseph: B-5, Joseph Kennedy, born 2 February 1883, baptized 8 February 1883, son of Louis Kennedy and Marie Sauteux, Godmother: Lizette Sauteux, Pierre St.Germain o.m.i. (page 2)

KENNEDY, Marie Christine: B-12, Marie Christine Kennedy, born 27 April 1900, baptized 14 May 1900, daughter of Henry Kennedy and Adele Malaterre, Godfather: Jean Marie McGillis, Godmother: Adele Dubreuil, Emmanuel Garon priest. (page 36)

KLYNE, Caroline: B-2, Caroline Klyne, born 12 January 1903, baptized 14 January 1903, daughter of Georges Klyne and Adele Gosselin, Godfather: William Klyne, Godmother: Caroline Klyne, C. J. Passaplan priest. (page 42)

KLYNE, Eloisa Marie: B-14, Eloisa Marie Klyne, born 19 August 1900, baptized 26 August 1900, daughter of Georges Klyne and Adele Gosselin, Godfather: Alexandre Gosselin, Godmother: Marie Champagne, Emmanuel Garon priest. (page 36)

KLYNE, Jean: Jean Klyne, son of George Klyne, age 3 months, buried 22 March 1906, M. Mesnage priest V. (page

139)

KLYNE, Joseph: B-8, Joseph Klyne, born 24 January 1883, baptized 12 February 1883, son of Joseph Klyne and Julie Flamand, Godfather: Joseph Desmarais, Godmother: Rosalie St.Denis, Pierre St.Germain o.m.i. (page 3)

KLYNE, Louise Anne: B-7, Louise Anne Klyne, born 11 April 1884, baptized 12 April 1884, daughter of William Klyne and Emerise Poitras, Godfather: Jean Louis Legare, Godmother: Emerise Lafournaise, Pierre St.Germain o.m.i. (page 6)

KLYNE, Marie Philomene: B-24, Marie Philomene Klyne, born 23 December 1885, baptized 25 December 1885, daughter of Guilluame Klyne and Madeleine Poitras, Godfather: Napolone Lafournaise, Godmother: Marie Theresa McGillis, Pierre St.Germain o.m.i. 15 April 1903 married Napoleon Rainville; 8 February 1931 married Joseph Racine. (page 9)

KLYNE, Philomene and Napoleon Carl RAINVILLE: M-1, Napoleon Carl Rainville, adult son of Hilaire Rainville and Seraphine Houle, married 15 April 1902, Philomene Klyne, minor daughter of Guilluame Klyne and Madeleine Poitras, Witness: Raymond Gosselin and Georges Klyne, Pierre St.Germain o.m.i. (page 114)

KLYNE, William: William Klyne, age 73, buried 8 January 1912, Alphonse Lemieux priest. (page 140)

KRUPPA, Joseph and Marie Bernadette ARCAND: M-4, Joseph Kruppa, son of Frank Kruppa and Juliana KJowaczs, married 3 November 1893, Marie Bernadette Arcand, daughter of of Alphee Arcand and Marie Anna Caroline Borne, Witnesses: Noel Paquin and Amada Paquin, Pierre St.Germain o.m.i. (page 112)

L'AOUT, Eglantine: Eglantine L'Aout, age 28, buried 8 February 1910, Witness: Alex L'Aout, Alphonse Lemieux priest. (page 140)

LACERTE, __: __ Lacerte (and baptism), buried 4 December 1899, Witness: Clement Lacerte, Emmanuel Garon priest. (page 138)

LACERTE, Albert: B-19, Albert Lacerte, born 8 December 1895, baptized 8 December 1895, son of Narcisse Lacerte and Seraphine Ouellette, A. Leuret priest. (page 27)

LACERTE, Catherine: B-14, Catherine Lacerte, born 22 October 1896, baptized 3 November 1896, daughter of Narcisse Lacerte and Seraphine Ouellette, Godfather: Clement Lacerte, Godmother: Emma Lacerte, Pierre St.Germain o.m.i. (page 29)

LACERTE, Clement and Eleanore OUELLETTE: M-1, Clement Lacerte, son of Narcisse Lacerte and Julie Caplette, married 9 May 1898, Eleonore Ouellette, daughter of Isidore Ouellette and Marie Botineau, Witness: Isidore Ouellette and Narcisse Lacerte, Pierre St.Germain o.m.i. (page 113)

LACERTE, Clement and Marie GOSSELIN: M-3, Clement Lacerte, widower of Eleonore Ouellette, son of Narcisse Lacerte and Julie Caplette, married 19 March 1906, Marie Gosselin, daughter of Antoine Gosselin and Helene Piche, Witness: Narcisse Lacerte and Octave Gosselin, Alphonse Lemieux priest. (page 115)

LACERTE, Emma: B-13, Emma Lacerte, born 9 September 1891, baptized 27 September 1891, daughter of Narcisse Lacerte and Seraphine Ouellette, Godfather: Narcisse Lacerte, Godmother: Julie Caplette, Pierre St.Germain o.m.i. (page 20)

LACERTE, Emma and Raymond GOSSELIN: M-1, Raymond Gosselin, son of Antoine Gosselin and Francoise

36

Delorme, married 22 January 1907, Emma Lacerte, daughter of Narcisse Lacerte and Seraphine Ouellette, Witness: Antoine Gosselin and Narcisse Lacerte, Alphonse Lemeiux priest. (page 115)

LACERTE, Florestine and Moise GAUDRY: M-2, Moise Gaudry, adult son of Andre Gaudry and Marie Beauchamp, married 3 June 1902, Florestine Lacerte, minor daughter of Narcisse Lacerte and Julie Caplette, Witness: _, C. Passaplan priest. (page 114)

LACERTE, Gregoire: B-18, Gregoire Lacerte, born 11 October 1904, baptized 14 October 1904, son of Narcisse Lacerte and Seraphine Ouellette, Godfather: Moise Gaudry, Godmother: Florestine Lacerte, C. J. Passaplan priest; married 20 April 1932 Marie Anna McGillis. (page 46)

LACERTE, Joseph: B-16, Joseph Lacerte, born 2 October 1907, baptized 6 October 1907, son of Narcisse Lacerte and Seraphine Ouellette, Godfather: Raymond Gosselin, Godmother: Emma Lacerte, Alphonse Lemieux priest; married 15 September 1931 Josephine Gosselin. (page 52)

LACERTE, Joseph Leon: B-4, Joseph Leon Lacerte, born 20 October 1898, baptized 30 October 1898, son of Narcisse Lacerte Jr. and Seraphine Ouellette, Godfather: Albert Legare, Godmother: Justine Piche, Emmanuel Garon priest. (page 32)

LACERTE, Joseph Leon: Joseph Leon Lacerte, age 2 months, died 10 January 1899, buried 14 January 1899, Witness: Narcisse Lacerte, Emmanuel Garon priest. (page 138)

LACERTE, Joseph Louis: B-6, Joseph Louis Lacerte, born 7 March 1899, baptized 7 March 1899, son of Clement Lacerte and Eleonore Ouellette, Godfather: Narcisse Lacerte, Godmother: Marie Botineau, Emmanuel Garon priest. (page 33)

LACERTE, Joseph Louis: Joseph Louis Lacerte, age 3 days, died 10 March 1899, buried 11 March 1899, Witness: Clement Lacerte, Emmanuel Garon priest. (page 138)

LACERTE, Josette and Joseph RIVARD: M-1, Joseph Rivard, son of Alexandre Rivard and Francoise Delorme, married 4 January 1910, Josette Lacerte, daughter of Narcisse Lacerte and Seraphine Ouellette, Witness: Alexandre Rivard and Narcisse Lacerte, Alphonse Lemieux priest. (page 116)

LACERTE, Jules: B-4, Jules Lacerte, born 19 March 1909, baptized 20 March 1909, son of Clement Lacerte and Marie Gosselin, Godfather: Louis Haggeyt, Godmother: Marie Roy, Alphonse Lemieux priest. (page 57)

LACERTE, Louis Clement: B-8, Louis Clement Lacerte, born 13 June 1907, baptized 16 June 1907, son of Clement Lacerte and Marie Gosselin, Godfather: Antoine Gosselin, Godmother: Helene Piche, Alphonse Lemieux; married 11 February 1929 Clemence Gosselin. (page 52)

LACERTE, Marguerite: B-11, Marguerite Lacerte, born 14 August 1889, baptized 17 August 1889, daughter of Narcisse Lacerte and Julie Caplette, Godfather: Jean Baptiste Caplette, Godmother: Josette Langer, Pierre St.Germain o.m.i. (page 17)

LACERTE, Marguerite: Marguerite Lacerte, age 3, died 19 March 1892, buried 20 March 1892, Witness: Clement Lacerte, Pierre St.Germain priest. (page 138)

LACERTE, Maria: B-2, Maria Lacerte, born 24 January 1902, baptized 25 January 1902, daughter of Clement Lacerte and Eleonore Ouellette, Godfather: Alexandre Ouellette, Godmother: Maria Lacerte, Pierre St.Germain o.m.i.; married 20 December 1919, Alfred Botineau. (page 39)

St.Ignace Parish of Willow Bunch, Saskatchewan
1882-1910, Baptisms, Marriages and Burials

LACERTE, Marie: B-29, Marie Lacerte, born 5 October 1886, baptized 31 October 1886, daughter of Narcisse Lacerte and Julie Caplette, Godfather: Guilllaume Klyne, Godmother: Madeleine Poitras, Pierre St.Germain o.m.i. (page 12)

LACERTE, Marie: B-7, Marie Lacerte, born 4 April 1902, baptized 6 April 1902, daughter of Narcisse Lacerte and Seraphine Ouellette, Godfather: Gaspard Beaupre, Godmother: Florestine Piche, Pierre St.Germain o.m.i. (page 40)

LACERTE, Marie and Jean Louis GOSSELIN: M-1, Jean Louis Gosselin, son of Alexandre Gosselin and Marie Champagne, married 10 January 1905, Marie Lacerte, daughter of Narcisse Lacerte and Julie Caplette, Witness: Narcisse Lacerte and Raymond Gosselin, C. J. Passaplan priest. (page 114)

LACERTE, Marie Josette: B-12, Marie Josette Lacerte, born 30 September 1893, baptized 1 October 1893, daughter of Narcisse Lacerte and Seraphine Ouellette, Godfather: Willliam John McGillis, Pierre St.Germain o.m.i.; married 12 January 1923, Patrice St.Denis. (page 23)

LACERTE, Marie Octavie: B-10, Marie Octavie Lacerte, born 12 March 1903, baptized 21 March 1903, daughter of Clement Lacerte and Eleonore Ouellette, Godfather: Louis Lapointe, Godmother: Marie Oman, C. J. Passaplan priest. (page 42)

LACERTE, Marie Seraphine: B-16, Marie Seraphine Lacerte, born 15 December 1889, baptized 16 December 1889, daughter of Narcisse Lacerte and Seraphine Ouellette, Godfather: Prudent Lapointe, Godmother: Elisabeth Ouellette, Pierre St.Germain o.m.i.; married 25 April 1910, Joseph McGillis. (page 17)

LACERTE, Narcisse and Seraphine OUELLETTE: M-1, Narcisse Lacerte, son of Narcisse Lacerte and Julie Caplette, married 8 January 1888, Seraphine Ouellette, daughter of Francois Ouellette and Josette Botineau, Witness: Isidore Ouellette and Joseph Short, Pierre St.Germain o.m.i. (page 111)

LACERTE, Narcisse: Narcisse Lacerte, age 63, buried 5 July 1909, Witness: Clement Lacerte, Alphonse Lemieux priest. (page 140)

LACERTE, Octavie: Octavie Lacerte, age 18, died 5 December 1897, buried 6 December 1897, Witness: Pierre Bruyere, Pierre St.Germain priest. (page 138)

LACERTE, Stella: Stella Lacerte, age 2, died 27 February 1904, buried, 29 February 1904, Witness: Jean Baptiste Caplette, C. J. Passaplan. (page 139)

LACERTE, Veronique: B-19, Veronique Lacerte, born 2 November 1900, baptized 2 November 1900, daughter of Clement Lacerte and Eleonore Ouellette, Godfather: Narcisse Lacerte Jr., Godmother: Seraphine Ouellette, Pierre St.Germain o.m.i. (page 37)

LACERTE, Veronique: Veronique Lacerte, age 6 months, buried 30 April 1901, Witness: Clement Lacerte, Pierre St.Germain priest. (page 139)

LACERTE, Virginie: Virginie Lacerte, age 15, died 8 June 1899, buried 10 June 1899, Witness: Narcisse Lacerte, Emmanuel Garon priest. (page 138)

LAFOURANISE, Elisa: B-26, Eloiza Lafournaise, born 5 August 1883, baptized 12 September 1883, daughter of Napoleon Lafournaise and Marie Therese McGillis, Godfather: Guilllaume Klyne, Godmother: Madeleine Poitras, Pierre St.Germain o.m.i. (page 4)

LAFOURNAISE, Emerise and Joseph OUELLETTE: M-2, Joseph Ouellette, son of Isidore Ouellette and Marie Botineau, married 18 May 1886, Emerise Lafournaise, daughter of Joseph Lafournaise and Madeleine Poitras, Witness: Francois Lafournaise and Prudent Lapointe, Pierre St.Germain. (page 111)

LAFOURNAISE, Francois: B-9, Francois Lafournaise, born 25 June 1897, baptized 25 July 1897, son of Napoleon Lafournaise and Therese McGillis, Godfather: Alexandre McGillis, Godmother: Marie Jeannotte, Pierre St.Germain o.m.i. (page 30)

LAFOURNAISE, Genevieve: B-27, Genevieve Lafouranise, born 15 January 1883, baptized 16 September 1883, daughter of Jean Baptiste Lafouranise and Caroline Cook, Godfather: Guillaume Klyne, Godmother: Emerise Lafournaise, Pierre St.Germain o.m.i. (page 4)

LAFOUNAISE, Joseph: Joseph Lafournaise, age 25, died 1 May 1883, buried 2 May 1883, Witness: Joseph Poitras, Pierre St.Germain priest. (page 137)

LAFOURNAISE, Joseph: B-23, Joseph Lafournaise, born 20 October 1885, baptized 29 November 1885, son of Jean Baptiste Lafournaise and Caroline Cook, Godfather: Jean Baptiste Amyot, Godmother: Genevieve Picard, Pierre St.Germain o.m.i. (page 9)

LAFOURNAISE, Joseph: Joseph Lafournaise, age 5, died 2 December 1891, buried 3 December 1891, Witness: Francois Lafournaise, Pierre St.Germain priest. (page 137)

LAFOURNAISE, Joseph Thomas: B-19, Joseph Thomas Lafournaise, born 19 December 1891, baptized 21 December 1891, son of Napoleon Lafournaise and Therese McGillis, Godfather: William Klyne, Godmother: Isabelle Fagnan, Pierre St.Germain o.m.i. (page 20)

LAFOURNAISE, Jude: B-8, Jude Lafournaise, born 27 June 1887, baptized 28 October 1887, son of Jean Baptiste Lafournaise and Caroline Cook, Godfather: Jean Plummer, Godmother: Catherine Cook, Pierre St.Germain o.m.i. (page 13)

LAFOURNAISE, Jude: Jude Laframboise, age 7 months, died 10 January 1888, buried 11 January 1888, Witness: Guillaume Klyne, Pierre St.Germain priest. (page 137)

LAFOURNAISE, Louisa: B-9, Louisa Lafournaise, born 8 August 1889, baptized 11 August 1889, daughter of Napoleon Lafournaise and Therese McGillis, Godfather: Alexandre McGillis, Godmother: Louise Anne Klyne, Pierre St.Germain o.m.i. (page 16)

LAFOURANISE, Marie and Louis DUBREUIL: M-3, Louis Dubreuil, adult son of Billy Dubreuil and Marie Malaterre, married 21 May 1900, Marie Lafournaise, minor daughter of Napoleon Lafournaise and Therese McGillis, Witness: Guilluame Klyne and Rev. Pierre St.Germain o.m.i., Emmanuel Garon priest. (page 113)

LAFOURNAISE, Marie Adeline: B-10, Marie Adeline Lafournaise, 15 August 1894, baptized 19 August 1894, daughter of Napoleon Lafournaise and Marie Therese McGillis, Godfather: Napoleon McGillis, Godmother: Philomene Fagnan, A. Leuret priest. (page 25)

LAFOURNAISE, Marie Josephine: B-4, Marie Josephine Lafournaise, born 11 February 1885, baptized 31 March 1885, daughter of Napoleon Lafournaise and Marie Therese McGillis, Godfather: Prudent Lapointe, Godmother: Marie Philomene McGillis, Pierre St.Germain o.m.i. (page 6)

LAFOURNAISE, Sarah: B-10, Sarah Lafouranise, born 23 September 1887, baptized 30 October 1887, daughter of Napoleon Lafournaise and Therese McGillis, Godfather: Georges Klyne, Godmother: Rose McGillis, Pierre St.Germain o.m.i.; married 10 July 1911, Albert Caplette. (page 14)

LAFRAMBOISE, Celina: Celina Laframboise, child of Gabriel Laframboise, age 12 years, buried 8 June 1911, A. Lemieux priest. (page 140)

LAFRAMBOISE, Marie Josephine: B-24, Marie Josephine Laframboise, born 11 April 1886, baptized 21 July 1886, daughter of Jean Baptiste Laframboise and Elise Thomas, Godfather: Napoleon Laframboise, Godmother: Marie Rose Villeneuve, Pierre St.Germain o.m.i. (page 12)

LAFRAMBOISE, Patrice: B-16, Patrice Laframboise, born 3 October 1885, baptized 4 June 1885, son of Francois Laframboise and Suzanne Rocheblanc, Godfather: David Boyer, Godmother: Louise Thomas, Pierre L. Legoff, priest o.m.i. (page 8)

LAFRAMBOISE, Patrice: B-25, Patrice Laframboise, born 27 June 1886, baptized 21 July 1886, son of Jean Laframboise and Marguerite Cayen, Godfather: Pascal Breland, Godmother: Rose McGillis, Pierre St.Germain o.m.i. (page 12)

LAFRAMBOISE, William: B-6, William Laframboise, born July 1884, baptized 22 May 1885, son of John Laframboise and Marguerite Cayen, Godfather: Michel St.Denis, Marie Laplante, Pierre St.Germain o.m.i. (page 6)

LAFRENIERE, Laurentia Aurore: B-24, Laurentia Aurore Lafrenierre, born 18 September 1909, baptized 19 September 1909, daughter of Rormisdas Lafreniere and Delvina Laporte, Godfather: Louis Beauchesne, Godmother: Lautina Miville, Alphonse Lemieux priest; married 18 November 1941 Alfred Rebat [?]. (page 59)

LALONDE, Albert: B-5, Albert Lalonde, born 21 January 1904, baptized 30 March 1904, son of Alfred Lalonde and Josephine Norman, Godfather: Georges Lalonde, Godmother: Anna Lalonde, C. J. Passaplan priest. (page 45)

LALONDE, Albert: Albert Lalonde, died 31 January [?] 1904, buried 30 March 1904, Witness: Theophile McGillis, C. J. Passaplan. (page 139)

LALONDE, Pascal Maurice: B-17, Pascal Maurice Lalonde, born 6 May 1908, baptized 14 June 1908, son of Alfred Lalonde and Josephine Normand, Godfather: Pascal Bonneau, Godmother: Widow Moudor, Alphonse Lemieux priest; married 21 November 1928, Marie Ange Charbonneau. (page 55)

LALONDE, Theodore: B-17, Theodore Lalonde, born 30 July 1906, baptized 26 August 1906, son of Alfred Lalonde and Josepine Norman, Godfather: Albert Sauvier, Godmother: Melina Sauvier, Alphonse Lemieux priest. (page 50)

LAMONTAGNE, Marie Alice Eva: B-16, Marie Alice Eva Lamantagne, born 17 July 1909, baptized 17 July 1909, daughter of Henri Lamontagne and Georgiana Letourneau, Godfather: Edouard de Laforest, Godmother: Elisa Letourneau, Alphonse Lemieux priest. (page 58)

LANDRY, Alexander: B-13, Alexander Landry, born 7 February 1883, baptized 4 March 1883, son of Maxime Landry and Marguerite Pelletier, Godfather: Pierre Landry, Isabelle Pelletier, Pierre St.Germain o.m.i. (page 3)

LANGER, Abraham: B-4, Abraham Langer, born February 1905, baptized February 1905, son of Bernard Langer and Marie Justine Gaudry, Godfather: Abraham Beauchamp, C. J. Passaplan priest. (page 47)

LANGER, Albert Eugene: B-15, Albert Eugene Langer, born 10 August 1904, baptized 14 August 1904, son of Alphonse Langer and Mathilde McGillis, Godfather: Albert Saulnier, Godmother: Melina Saulnier, C. J. Passaplan priest. (page 46)

LANGER, Alfred: B-6, Alfred Langer, born 4 June 1887, baptized 12 June 1887, son of David Langer and Marie Page, Godfather: Hilaire Rainville, Godmother: Elisa Caplette, Pierre St.Germain o.m.i. (page 13)

LANGER, Alphonse and Mathilda MCGILLIS: M-1, Alphonse Langer, adult son of David Langer and Marie Page, married 8 April 1901, Mathilda McGillis, adult daughter of Modeste McGillis and Isabelle Poitras, Witness: Pierre Briere and Francois Lafournaise, Pierre St.Germain o.m.i. (page 113)

LANGER, Alphonse Raphael: B-16, Alphonse Raphael Langer, born 14 August 1906, baptized 21 August 1906, son of Alphonse Langer and Mathilde McGillis, Godfather: Jean Marie Whiteford, Godmother: Marie Genevieve Whiteford, Alphonse Lemieux priest. (page 50)

LANGER, Bernard and Marie GAUDRY: M-1, Bernard Langer, adult son of David Langer and Marie Page, married 30 January 1900, Marie Gaudry, adult daughter of Andre Gaudry and Marie Beauchamp, Witness: Andre Gaudry and Treffle Bonneau, Emmanuel Garon priest. (page 113)

LANGER, Bernard: Bernard Langer, died 2 April 1904, buried 2 April 1904, Witness: Bernard Langer, C. J. Passaplan. (page 139)

LANGER, Bernard: Bernard Langer, age 27 [?], died 2 March 1911, buried 5 March 1911, Lemieux priest. (page 140)

LANGER, Celina: Celina Langer, age 30, buried 3 July 1915, Alphonse Lemieux priest. (page 141)

LANGER, David: B-14, David Langer, born 23 September 1889, baptized 24 September 1889, son of David Langer and Marie Page, Godfather: Francois Lafournaise, Godmother: Marie Desjardins, Pierre St.Germain o.m.i. (page 17)

LANGER, David: David Langer, age 8 months, buried 5 June 1890, Witness: Alexandre McGillis, Pierre St.Germain priest. (page 137)

LANGER, David: David Langer, age 87, buried 4 May 1916, Alphonse Lemieux priest. (page 142)

LANGER, Ernestine: B-28, Ernestine Langer, born 6 August 1883, baptized 16 September 1883, daughter of Jean Baptiste Langer and Justine Malaterre, Godfather: Joseph Charette, Godmother: Rosalie Colin, Pierre St.Germain o.m.i. (page 5)

LANGER, Florestine: B-7, Florestine Langer, born 22 February 1903, baptized 24 February 1903, daughter of Bernard Langer and Marie Justine Gaudry, Godfather: Moise Gaudry, Godmother: Florestine _ [Lacerte], C. J. Passaplan priest, married Lebret 3 May 1932 J. Zacharie Blondeau. (page 42)

LANGER, Francois Xavier: B-11, Francois Xavier Langer, born 15 June 1906, baptized 16 June 1906, son of Bernard Langer and Marie Gaudry, Godfather: Francois Gervais, Godmother: Cecile Gervais, Alphonse Lemieux, priest. (page 50)

LANGER, Francois Xavier: B-22, Francois Xavier Langer, born 3 September 1908, baptized 6 September 1908, son of Alphonse Langer and Mathilde McGillis, Godfather: Francois Xavier Langer, Godmother: Josephine Boxeur, Alphonse Lemieux priest. (page 55)

LANGER, Jean Baptiste: B-1, Jean Baptiste Langer, born 18 January 1902, baptized 18 January 1902, son of Alphonse Langer and Mathilde McGillis, Godfather: Modeste McGillis, Godmother: Isabelle Poitras, Pierre St.Germain o.m.i. (page 39)

LANGER, Jean Baptiste: Jean Baptiste Langer, age 3 months, died 11 April 1902, buried 12 April 1902, Witness: Pierre Dumont, Pierre St.Germain priest. (page 139)

LANGER, Joseph: Joseph Langer, age _, died 29 December 1889, buried 30 December 1889, Witness: Joseph Hamelin, Pierre St.Germain priest. (page 137)

LANGER, Julienne: Julienne Langer, age 20, died 5 June 1902, buried 5 June 1902, Witness: David Langer, J. P. Magnon. (page 139)

LANGER, Marie Celina and Jimmy WHITEFORD: M-3, Jimmy Whiteford, son of Jimmy Whiteford and Sarah Gladu, married 14 October 1907, Marie Celina Langer, daughter of David Langer and Marie Page, Witness: David Langer and Jean Baptiste Whiteford, Alphonse Lemieux priest. (page 115)

LANGER, Marie Julienne: B-11, Marie Julienne Langer, born 7 August 1907, baptized 11 August 1907, daughter of Bernard Langer and Marie Gaudry, Godfather: Amable Gaudry, Godmother: Marie Langer, Arthur Magnan priest. (page 52)

LANGER, Marie Virginie: B-7, Marie Virginie Langer, born 30 June 1894, baptized 1 July 1894, daughter of Antoine Langer and Elisa Hainault, Godfather: Prudent Lapointe, Godmother: Ernestine Briere, A. Leuret priest. (page 24)

LANGER, Marius: B-5, Marius Langer, born 19 January 1903, baptized 21 January 1903, son of Alphonse Langer and Mathilde McGillis, Godfather: Joseph Langer, Godmother: Marguerite McGillis, C. J. Passaplan priest. (page 42)

LANGER, Raphael Andre : B-12, Raphael Andre Langer, born 23 October 1901, baptized 24 October 1901, son of Bernard Langer and Marie Gaudry, Godfather: Andre Gaudry, Godmother: Marie Beauchamp, Pierre St.Germain o.m.i. (page 39)

LANGER, Raphael: Raphael Langer, age 8 days, died 1 November 1901, buried 2 November 1901, Witness: Bernard Langer, Pierre St.Germain priest. (page 139)

LANGER, Willie: B-27, Willie Langer, born 28 October 1908, baptized 29 October 1908, son of Bernard Langer and Marie Gaudry, Godfather: Louis Paquin, Godmother: Marie Helene Chartrand, Alphonse Lemieux priest. (page 56)

LANGER, Willie: Willie Langer, infant of Bernard Langer, age 11 months, buried 1 October 1909, Alphonse Lemieux priest. (page 140)

LANGER, Xavier: Xavier Langer, age 39, buried 1 December 1910, A. Lemieux priest. (page 140)

LAPLANTE, Antoine Louis: B-14, Antoine Louis Laplante, born 29 June 1906, baptized 7 July 1906, son of Louis Laplante and Virginie Fleury, Godfather: Joseph Laplante, Godmother: Louise Lavallee [Leveille], M. Mesnage vic. (page 50)

LAPLANTE, Joseph Pierre: B-31, Joseph Pierre Plante (Laplante), born 7 November 1908, baptized 8 November 1908, son of Joseph Plante and Louise Leveille, Godfather: Patrice St.Denis, Godmother: Marguerite Sauve, Alphonse Lemieux priest. (page 56)

LAPLANTE, Joseph Pierre: B-34, Joseph Pierre Laplante, born 7 November 1908, baptized 8 November 1908, son of Joseph Laplante and Louise Leveille, Godfather: Patrice St.Denis, Godmother: Marguerite Sauve, Alphonse Lemieux priest. (page 56)

LAPLANTE, Louis: Louis Laplante, buried 26 July 1904, Witness: Louis Laplante, C. J. Passaplan. (page 139)

LAPLANTE, Louis Albert: Louis Albert Lapointe, age 7 months, buried 12 Dec 1910, A. Lemieux priest. (page 140)

LAPLANTE, Marie Josette: B-8, Marie Josette Laplante, born 8 April 1906, baptized 9 April 1906, daughter of Joseph Laplante and Louise Leveille, Godfather: Louis Joseph Haggeyt, Godmother: Marie Roy, Alphonse Lemieux priest. (page 49)

LAPLANTE, Rosalie: B-4, Rosalie Laplante, born 5 January 1904, baptized 28 February 1904, daughter of Joseph Laplante and Louise Leveille, Godfather: Louis Roy, Godmother: Josette Roy, C. J. Passaplan priest. (page 44)

LAPOINTE, Albert and Marguerite ROY: M-2, Albert Lapointe, son of Prudent Lapointe and Elisabeth Ouellette, married 20 April 1909, Marguerite Roy, daughter of Louis Roy and Marguerite Sauve, Witness: Louis Roy and Prudent Lapointe, Alphonse Lemieux priest. (page 116)

LAPOINTE, Alfred: B-11, Alfred Lapointe, born 24 September 1894, baptized 30 September 1894, son of Joseph Lapointe and Elise Ouellette, Godfather: William Klyne, Godmother: Madeleine Poitras, A. Leuret priest. (page 25)

LAPOINTE, Alfred: Alfred Lapointe, died 29 March 1895, buried 20 March 1895, Witness: family, A. Lerch priest. (page 138)

LAPOINTE, Gaspard: Gaspard Lapointe, age 13 months, died 14 September 1900, buried 15 September 1900, Witness: Prudent Lapointe, Pierre St.Germain priest. (page 138)

LAPOINTE, Jean Louis: B-12, Jean Louis Lapointe, born 15 March 1908, baptized 20 March 1908, son of Prudent Lapointe and Elisabeth Ouellette, Godfather: Louis Lapointe, Godmother: Francois Landry, Alphonse Lemieux priest; married 26 October 1935 Amelia Gareau. (page 54)

LAPOINTE, Joseph: B-14, Joseph Lapointe, born 9 November 1887, baptized 13 November 1887, son of Prudent Lapointe and Elisabeth Ouellette, Godfather: Joseph Lapointe, Godmother: Elisa Ouellette, Pierre St.Germain o.m.i. (page 14)

LAPOINTE, Joseph: Joseph Lapointe, age 6 months, died 20 May 1888, buried 21 May 1888, Witness: Gaspard Beaupre, Joseph St.Germain priest. (page 137)

LAPOINTE, Joseph and Eloisa OUELLETTE: M-1, Joseph Lapointe, son of Louis Lapointe and Adele Dugas, married 16 July 1885, Eloisa Ouellette, daughter of Isidore Ouellette and Marie Botineau, Witness: _, Pierre St.Germain o.m.i. (page 111)

LAPOINTE, Joseph Emile: Joseph Emile Lapointe, age 7 months, died 17 December 1891, buried 18 December 1891, Witness: Isidore Ouellette, Pierre St.Germain priest. (page 137)

LAPOINTE, Joseph Marie: B-10, Joseph Marie Lapointe, born 6 December 1892, baptized 8 December 1892, son of Joseph Lapointe and Elisa Ouellette, Godfather: James Ouellette, Godmother: Felicite Lafournaise, Pierre St.Germain o.m.i. (page 21)

LAPOINTE, Joseph Marie Emile: B-11, Joseph Marie Emile Lapointe, born 27 June 1891, baptized 28 June 1891, son of Joseph Lapointe and Elisa Ouellette, Godfather: Gaspard Beaupre, Godmother: Florestine Piche, Pierre St.Germain o.m.i. (page 20)

LAPOINTE, Joseph Oscar: B-12, Joseph Oscar Lapointe, born 31 July 1899, baptized 10 September 1899, son of Prudent Lapointe and Elisabeth Ouellette, Godfather: Gaspard Beaupre, Godmother: Florestine Piche, Emmanuel Garon priest. (page 34)

LAPOINTE, Joseph Treffle: B-9, Joseph Treffle Lapointe, born 20 April 1893, baptized 20 April 1893, son of Prudent Lapointe and Elisabeth Ouellette, Godfather: Treffle Bonneau, Godmother: Marie Louise Vaudry, Pierre St.Germain o.m.i. (page 23)

LAPOINTE, Joseph Treffle: Joseph Treffle Lapointe, age 2 months, buried 2 July 1893, Witness: Joseph Short, Pierre St.Germain priest. (page 138)

LAPOINTE, Jules: B-8, Jules Lapointe, born 25 July 1894, baptized 12 August 1894, son of Prudent Lapointe and Elisabeth Ouellette, Godfather: Joseph Botineau, Godmother: Eleonore Ouellette, A. Leuret priest. (page 24)

LAPOINTE, Jules: Jules Lapointe, infant, died 10 April 1901, buried 11 April 1901, Witness: Prudent Lapointe, Pierre St.Germain priest. (page 139)

LAPOINTE, Leon: B-2, Leon Lapointe, born 16 April 1890, baptized 17 April 1890, son of Joseph Lapointe and Elisa Ouellette, Godfather: Elzear Botineau, Godmother: Isabelle Botineau, Pierre St.Germain o.m.i.; married 15 August 1911, Elise Laroque. (page 18)

LAPOINTE, Louis: B-11, Louis Lapointe, born 19 September 1887, baptized 30 October 1887, son of Joseph Lapointe and Eloiza Ouellette, Godfather: Prudent Lapointe, Godmother: Eleonore Ouellette, Pierre St.Germain o.m.i., married 12 April 1910, Emerence Gosselin. (page 14)

LAPOINTE, Lucie Catherine: B-16, Lucie Catherine Lapointe, born 23 November 1897, baptized 25 November 1897, daughter of Joseph Lapointe and Elisa Ouellette, Godfather: Louis Dumais, Godmother: Marie Rose Lapointe, Pierre St.Germain o.m.i.; married 6 December 1822, Pierre Paulhus, died February 1967, married Eugene Desnoyers at Weyburn. (page 31

LAPOINTE, Marie: Marie Lapointe, age _, died 1 October 1889, buried 2 October 1889, Witness: Elzeard Botineau, Pierre St.Germain priest. (page 137)

LAPOINTE, Marie Josephine: B-2, Marie Josephine Lapointe, born 29 March 1889, baptized 30 March 1889, daughter of Joseph Lapointe and Elisa Ouellette, Godfather: Joseph Short, Godmother: Josette Botineau, Pierre St.Germain o.m.i. (page 16)

LAPOINTE, Marie Louise: B-6, Marie Louise Lapointe, born 26 May 1891, baptized 30 May 1891, daughter of Prudent Lapointe and Elisabeth Ouellette, Godfather: Joseph Short, Godmother: Josette Botineau, Pierre St.Germain o.m.i.; married, 13 May 1913, Francois Boxeur. (page 19)

St.Ignace Parish of Willow Bunch, Saskatchewan
1882-1910, Baptisms, Marriages and Burials

LAPOINTE, Marie Madeleine: B-4, Marie Madeleine Lapointe, born 12, March 1901, baptized 17 March 1901, daughter of Prudent Lapointe and Elisabeth Ouellette, Godfather: Moise Ouellette, Godmother: Madeleine Pelletier, Pierre St.Germain o.m.i.; married 22 November 1922, Jean Bouldayes. (page 38)

LAPOINTE, Marie Rose: B-26, Marie Rose Lapointe, born 25 July 1886, baptized 13 August 1886, daughter of Joseph Lapointe and Elisa Ouellette, Godfather: Isidore Ouellette, Godmother: Marie Botineau, Pierre St.Germain o.m.i. married, 12 July 1912 Joseph Mariotte. (page 12)

LAPOINTE, Marie Rosina: B-8, Marie Rosina Lapointe, born 2 March 1903, baptized 2 March 1903, daughter of Joseph Lapointe and Laiza Ouellette, Godfather: Clement Lacerte, Godmother: Angelique Chartrand, C. J. Passaplan priest. (page 42)

LAPOINTE, Nathalie Rose: B-13, Nathalie Rose Lapointe, born 10 July 1904, baptized 10 July 1904, daughter of Prudent Lapointe and Elisabeth Ouellette, Godfather: Francois Boxeur, Godmother: Elise McGillis, C. J. Passaplan priest. (page 45)

LAPOINTE, Prudent and Elisabeth OUELLETTE: M-3, Prudent Lapointe, son of Louis LaPointe and Adele Dugas, married 7 July 1886, Elisabeth Ouellette, daughter of Francois Ouellette and Josette Botineau, Witness: Isidore Ouellette and Joseph Lapointe, Pierre St.Germain o.m.i. (page 111)

LAPOINTE, Prudent Albert: B-6, Prudent Albert Lapointe, born 10 June 1889, baptized 16 June 1889, son of Prudent Lapointe and Elisabeth Ouellette, Godfather: Narcisse Lacerte Jr., Godmother: Saraphine Ouellette, Pierre St.Germain o.m.i.; married, 20 April 1909, Marguerite Roy. (page 16)

LAPOINTE, Rosalie: Rosalie Lapointe, age 6 months, died 10 August 1900, buried 11 August 1900, Witness: Joseph Lapointe, Pierre St.Germain priest. (page 138)

LAPOINTE, Virginie: B-28, Virginie Lapointe, born 19 November 1909, baptized 21 November 1909, daughter of Prudent Lapointe and Elisabeth Ouellette, Godfather: Albert Lapointe, Godmother: Marguerite Roy, Alphonse Lemieux priest. (page 59)

LAPOINTE, Zacharie: B-16, Zacharie Lapointe, born 15 August 1896, baptized 8 November 1896, son of Prudent Lapointe and Elisabeth Ouellette, Godfather: Zacharie Chartrand, Godmother: Victoire Breland, Pierre St.Germain o.m.i. (page 29)

LAPOINTE, Zacharie: Zacharie Lapointe, died 2 March 1897, buried 12 March 1897, Witness: Louis Roy, Pierre St.Germain priest. (page 138)

LAROCQUE, Albert: B-4, Albert Larocque, born 23 May 1889, baptized 25 May 1889, son of Louis Larocque and Sarah Gosselin, Godfather: Alexander Gosselin, Godmother: Adele Gosselin, Pierre St.Germain o.m.i. (page 16)

LAROCQUE, Elise: B-8, Elise Larocque, born 29 May 1891, baptized 2 June 1891, daughter of Louis Larocque and Sarah Gosselin, Godfather: Francois Caplette, Godmother: Elisa Gosselin, Pierre St.Germain o.m.i.; married 15 August 1911, Leon Lapointe. (page 19)

LAROCQUE, Francois: B-18, Francois Larocque, born 12 June 1908, baptized 14 June 1908, son of Louison Larocque and Sarah Gosselin, Godfather: Louis Lapointe, Godmother: Elise Larocque, A. Lemieux priest; married 3 February 1932 Catherine Short. (page 55)

LAROCUQE, Joseph and Philomene ST.DENIS: M-2, Joseph Larocque, son of Baptiste Larocque and Julie

St.Ignace Parish of Willow Bunch, Saskatchewan
1882-1910, Baptisms, Marriages and Burials

Lemieux, married 14 October 1895, Philomene St.Denis, daughter of Pierre St.Denis and Adelaide Dauphinais, Witness: Isidore Ouellette and Antoine Caplette, Albert Leuret priest. (page 113)

LAROCUQE, Joseph Alfred: B-18, Joseph Alfred Larocque, born 10 December 1905, baptized 26 December 1905, son of Louison Larocque and Sarah Gosselin, Godfather: Francois Gosselin, Godmother: Emerence Gosselin, Alphonse Lemieux priest. (page 48)

LAROCQUE, Joseph Louis: B-9, Joseph Louis Larocque, born 22 April 1900, baptized 24 April 1900, son of Louis Larocque, Sarah Gosselin, Godfather: Pierre Briere, Godmother: Helene Gosselin, Emmanuel Garon priest. (page 36)

LAROCQUE, Louis and Sarah GOSSELIN: M-1, Louis Larocque, son of Louis Larocque and Suzanne Ledoux, married 16 February 1886, Sarah Gosselin, daughter of Alexandre Gosselin and Marie Champagne, Witness: Joseph Lapointe and Bernard Hamelin, Pierre St.Germain o.m.i. (page 111)

LAROCQUE, Marie Amelie: B-21, Marie Amelie Larocque, born 23 September 1902, baptized 28 September 1902, daughter of Louison Larocque and Sarah Gosselin, Godfather: Louis Briere, Godmother: Josette Berard, C. J. Passaplan priest; married 28 November 1928 Edmond Oscar Lesperance. (page 41)

LAROCQUE, Marie Josephine: B-2, Marie Josephine Larocque, born 12 March 1898, baptized 5 May 1898, daughter of Louis Larocque and Sarah Gosselin, Godfather: Andre Gaudry, Godmother: Marie Beauchamp, Pierre St.Germain o.m.i.; married 3 February 1922, Edouard Baudin. (page 32)

LAROCQUE, Marie Julie: B-13, Marie Julie Larocque, born July 1899, baptized 16 September 1899, daughter of Joseph Larocque and Philomene St.Denis, Godfather: Pierre Larocque, Emmanuel Garon priest. (page 34)

LAROCQUE, Patrice: B-3, Patrice Larocque, born 6 May 1887, baptized 7 May 1887, son of Louis Larocque and Sarah Gosselin, Godfather: William Beston, Godmother: Marie Rose Gosselin, Pierre St.Germain o.m.i. (page 13)

LAROCQUE, Virginie: B-15, Virginie Larocque, born 19 August 1893, baptized 9 October 1893, daughter of Louis Larocque and Sarah Gosselin, Godfather: Alexandre Gosselin Sr., Godmother: Marie Champagne, Pierre St.Germain o.m.i.; married, 23 July 1922, William Klyne. (page 23)

LASANTE, Marie Louise: B-10, Marie Louise Lasante, born 24 August 1901, baptized 19 September 1901, daughter of Louis Lasante and Caroline Plummer, Godfather: Andre Gaudry, Godmother: Marie Beauchamp, Pierre St.Germain o.m.i. (page 38)

LAUTIER, Leon Jules: B-19, Leon Jules Lautier, born 15 October 1907, baptized 24 November 1907, son of Jules Lautier and Clementine Thierrin, Godfather: Leon Curral, Godmother: Maria Lautier, Alphonse Lemieux priest. (page 53)

LAUTIER, Mraia and Leon CURRAT: M-4, Leon Currat, son of Antoine Currat (Swiss) and Reine _, married 29 October 1906, Maria Lautier, daughter of Raymond Lautier and Francoise Blanche, Witness: Alfred Currat and Virginie Chartrand, Alphonse Lemieux priest. (page 115)

LAVALLEE, Marie Alice Cecile: B-25, Marie Alice Cecile Lavallee, born 6 October 1908, baptized 7 October 1908, daughter of Arthur Lavallee and Anna Legare, Godfather: Albert Legare, Godmother: Justine Piche, Alphonse Lemieux priest; married 14 April 1936 Mederic Forest. (page 55)

LAVERDURE, Elie: B-19, Elie Laverdure, born 5 March 1886, baptized 30 May 1886, son of Francois Laverdure

46

St.Ignace Parish of Willow Bunch, Saskatchewan
1882-1910, Baptisms, Marriages and Burials

and Marie Turcotte, Godfather: Vital Turcotte, Godmother: Adele Berger, Pierre St.Germain o.m.i. (page 11)

LEDUC, Charles Leon: B-20, Charles Leon Leduc, born 6 June 1908, baptized 9 August 1908, son of Raymond Leduc and Lucie Aussapt, Godfather: Leon Currat, Godmother: Berthe Leduc, Alphonse Lemieux priest. (page 55)

LEDUE, Armandien Helene: B-22, Armandien Helene Ledue, born 9 March 1909, baptized 19 March 1909, daughter of Rene Ledue and Berthe Durand, Godfather: Raymond Ledue, Godmother: Helene Perthuis, Alphonse Lemieux priest. (page 59)

LEDOUX, Louis: B-10, Louis Ledoux, born 25 July 1882, baptized 27 December 1882, son of Napoleon Ledoux and Caroline Thomas, Godfather: Louis Dumais, Godmother: Eloize Caplette, Pierre St.Germain o.m.i. (page 2)

LEGARE, Catherine: B-8, Catherine Legare, born 14 April 1902, baptized 20 April 1902, daughter of Albert Legare and Justine Piche, Godfather: Narcisse Lacerte Jr., Godmother: Seraphine Ouellette, Pierre St.Germain o.m.i.; married Assiniboia, 30 December 1928 [?], Joseph Marcotte. (page 40)

LEGARDE, Jean Gedeon: B-13, Jean Gedeon Legare, born 30 September 1897, baptized 17 November 1897, son of Albert Legare and Justine Piche, Godfather: Jean Louis Legare, Godmother: Cecile Desmarais, Pierre St.Germain o.m.i. (page 31)

LEGARE, Joseph Marius: B-7, Joseph Marius Legare, born 14 April 1900, baptized 15 April 1900, son of Albert Legare and Justine Piche, Godfather: Antoine Gosselin, Godmother: Helene Piche, Emmanuel Garon priest; married 31 January 1918, Mathilda Beston. (page 35)

LEGARE, Maria: Maria Legare, age 9 days, died 28 April 1899, buried 29 April 1899, Witness: Albert Legare, Emmanuel Garon priest. (page 138)

LEGARE, Maria Lida: B-8, Maria Lida Legare, born 19 April 1899, baptized 27 April 1899, daughter of Albert Legare and Justine Piche, Godfather: Gaspard Beaupre, Godmother: Florestine Piche, Emmanuel Garon priest. (page 33)

LEGARE, Marie Anne Justine: B-6, Marie Anne Justine Legare, born 23 February 1908, baptized 25 February 1908, daughter of Albert Legare and Justine Piche, Godfather: Arthur Leveille, Godmother: Anna Legare, Alphonse Lemieux priest. (page 54)

LEGARE, Marie Louise: Marie Louise Legare, wife of Louis Granger, age 60, buried 7 August 1909, Alphonse Lemieux priest. (page 140)

LEGARE, Oscar: B-20, Oscar Legare, born 3 November 1904, baptized 6 November 1904, son of Albert Legare and Justine Piche, Godfather: Joseph Hamelin, Godmother: Philomene Piche, C. J. Passaplan priest. (page 46)

LEMAIRE, Clotilde Julia: B-10, Clotilde Julia Lemaire, born 18 December 1908, baptized 6 June 1909, daughter of Lucien Lemaire and Julia Fastier, Godfather: Jean Baptiste Caplette, Godmother: Rose Anne Venne, Alphonse Lemieux priest. (page 57)

LEMIRE, Francois Xavier: B-8, Francois Xavier Lemire, born 14 November 1882, baptized 6 December 1882, son of Francois Xavier Lemire and _, Godfather: Francois Desjarlais, Godmother: Josette Pelletier, Pierre St.Germain o.m.i. (page 1)

LEMIRE, Joseph: B-20, Joseph Lemire, born March 1883, baptized 7 May 1883, son of Carpel [Cuthbert] Lemire and Louise Swain, Godfather: Pierre Emmery, Godmother: Melanie Pelletier, Pierre St.Germain o.m.i. (page 4)

LERAT, Alexandre: B-12, Alexandre Lerat (Illegitimate), born 13 February 1883, baptized 27 February 1883, son of Francois LeRatand Amelie Desjarlais, Godfather: Alexander Fisher, Godmother: Elisabeth Pelletier, Pierre St.Germain o.m.i.

LESPERANCE, Alexis Edouard: B-2, Alexis Edouard Lesperance, born 5 January 1906, baptized 10 January 1906, son of Edouard Lesperance and Josephine Beaupre, Godfather: Francois Gervais, Godmother: Cecile Desmarais, Alphonse Lemieux priest; married 27 December 1929 Marie Laure Lavallee. (page 49)

LESPERANCE, Edmond and Josephine BEAUPRE: M-1, Edmond Lesperance, born 15 January 1880 SFX, son of Alexandre Lesperance and Cleophee Page, married 5 January 1904, Josephine Beaupre, daughter of Gaspard Beaupre and Florestine Piche, Witness: Hormidas Granger and Alexandre Briere, C. J. Passaplan priest. (page 114)

LESPERANCE, Edmond Oscar Julien: B-12, Edmond Oscar Julien Lesperance, born 16 August 1907, baptized 19 August 1907, son of Edmon and Josephine Beaupre, Godfather: Alphonse Dauphinais, Godmother: Adelaide Lesperance, Arthur Magnan priest; married 1) 28 November 1928 Marie Amelie Laroque, married 2) 3 October 1933 Marie Degana. (page 52)

LESPERANCE, Eugene: Eugene Lesperance, infant of Edmond Lesperance, age 8 months, buried 18 April 1910, Alphonse Lemieux priest. (page 140)

LESPERANCE, Joseph Eugene Adelard Denis: B-19, Joseph Eugene Adelard Denis Leesperance, born 19 August 1909, baptized 22 August 1909, son of Edmond Lesperance and Josephine Beaupre, Godfather: Alfred Beaupre, Godmother: Eva Lesperance, Alphonse Lemieux priest. (page 58)

LESPERANCE, Marie: B-22, Marie Lesperance, born 2 December 1904, baptized 4 December 1904, daughter of Edmond Lesperance and Josephine Beaupre, Godfather: Gaspard Beaupre, Godmother: Florestine Piche, C. J. Passaplan priest. (page 46)

LESPERANCE, Marie: Marie Lesperance, daughter of Edmond Lesperance, age 3, buried 28 December 1907, Alphonse Lemieux priest. (page 139)

LETILLY, Marie Louise Alexandrine: B-7, Marie Louise Alexandrine Letilly, born 6 September 1908, baptized 1 May 1909, daughter of Jean Letilly and Marie Mathurine Gearguen, Godfather: Alexandre Letilly, Godmother: Leonine Ledozzy, Alphonse Lemieux priest. (page 57)

LEVEILLE, Paul: B-10, Paul Leveille, born 5 December 1885, baptized 30 March 1886, son of Paul Leveille and Rosalie Pelletier, Godfather: Norbert Poitras, Godmother: Elisa Boyer, Pierre St.Germain o.m.i. (page 10)

MABLE, Laiza: B-10, Laiza Mable, born 23 January 1904, baptized 25 June 1904, daughter of Henry Mable and Lina Malette (non-Catholic), Godfather: Jean Baptiste Caplette, Godmother: Flore Caplette, C. J. Passaplan priest. (page 45)

MACA-TIBI, Joseph: B-7, Joseph Maca-tibi (Sioux), age 60 years, baptized 21 June 1889, Godfather: Gaspard Beaupre, Pierre St.Germain, o.m.i. (page 16)

MACA-TINI, Marie: B-4, Marie Maca-tini (Indian), born 1878, baptized 15 July 1888, Parents Indian, Godfather: Andre Gaudry, Pierre St.Germain o.m.i. (page 15)

St.Ignace Parish of Willow Bunch, Saskatchewan
1882-1910, Baptisms, Marriages and Burials

MALASUER, Frederic: Frederic Malasuer, age 6, died 27 June 1886, buried 27 June 1886, Witness: Ambroise Blondeau, Pierre St.Germain priest. (page 137)

MALATERRE, Edouard: B-6, Edouard Malaterre, born 23 March 1884, baptized 23 March 1884, son of Jeremie Malaterre and Alphonsine Ouellette, Godfather: Elzear Botineau, Godmother: Josette Botineau, Pierre St.Germain o.m.i. (page 6)

MALATERRE, Louis Napoleon: B-36, Louis Napoleon Malaterre, born 31 October 1883, baptized 1 November 1883, son of Zacharie Malaterre and Rebecca Ouellette, Godfather: Alexis Malaterre, Godmother: Marguerite Ward, Pierre St.Germain o.m.i. (page 5)

MALATERRE, Marie Virginie: B-13, Marie Virginie Malaterre, born 6 May 1886, baptized 7 May 1886, daughter of Jeremie Malaterre and Alphonsine Ouellette, Godfather: Jean Louis Legare, Godmother: Alphonsine Ouellette, Pierre St.Germain (page 11)

MALATERRE, Rosine: B-7, Rosine Malaterre, born 28 March 1892, baptized 10 July 1892, daughter of Charles Malaterre and Isabelle Rocheblave, Godfather: Louis Plante, Godmother: Guillelmine Fagnon, Pierre St.Germain o.m.i. (page 21)

MALBOEUF, Eloiza: Eloiza Malboeuf, age 5, buried 7 May 1883, Witness: Raphael Pelletier, Pierre St.Germain priest. (page 137)

MALBOEUF, Joseph Alfred: B-18, Joseph Alfred Malboeuf, born 8 August 1882, baptized 7 May 1883, son of Pierre Malboeuf and Marie Ross, Godfather: Charles Delorme, Godmother: Isabelle Piche, Pierre St.Germain o.m.i. (page 4)

MARION, Marie Rose: B-6, Marie Rose Marion, born 31 January 1883, baptized 8 February 1883, daughter of Norman Marion and Rose Ouellette, Godfather: Charles Champagne, Godmother: Marie Ouellette, Pierre St.Germain o.m.i. (page 2)

MARTIN, Clara: B-15, Clara Martin, born 15 November 1901, baptized 21 July 1902, daughter of Gilbert Martin and Marie Clemence Simpson, Godfather: Joseph Simpson, Godmother: Sarah Simpson, C. J. Passaplan priest. (page 41)

Alexander MCGILLIS
Alexandre McGillis, age 23, died 18 September 1901, buried 19 September 1901, Witness: Alexandre McGillis, Pierre St.Germain priest. (page 139)

Alfred Robert MCGILLIS
B-15, Alfred Robert McGillis, born 14 November 1901, baptized 16 November 1901, son of Gregoire McGillis and Helene Gosselin, Godfather: Jean Marie McGillis, Godmother: Adele Dubreuil, Pierre St.Germain; married 7 July 1926 Annie Salaba [?]. (page 39)

MCGILLIS, Angus: Angus McGillis, age _, died 1 May 1888, buried 2 May 1888, Witness: Louis Legare, Pierre St.Germain priest. (page 137)

MCGILLIS, Antoine: B-2, Antoine McGillis, born 16 February 1901, baptized 17 February 1901, son of Jean Marie McGillis and Adele Dubreuil, Godfather: Antoine Caplette, Godmother: Athalie Trottier, Pierre St.Germain o.m.i. (page 38)

St.Ignace Parish of Willow Bunch, Saskatchewan
1882-1910, Baptisms, Marriages and Burials

MCGILLIS, Antoine: Antoine McGillis, age 3 months, died 14 April 1902, buried 15 April 1902, Witness: Alexandre McGillis, Pierre St.Germain priest. (page 139)

MCGILLIS, Elise and Francois BOXEUR: M-4, Francois Boxeur, son of Joseph Boxeur and Julie Sauteuse, married 7 June 1886, Elise McGillis, daughter of Modeste McGillis and Isabelle Poitras, Witness: Andre Gaudry and Isidore Ouellette, Pierre St.Germain o.m.i. (page 111)

MCGILLIS, Florestine: Florestine McGillis, age 3, buried 21 March 1891, Witness: Antoine Morin, Pierre St.Germain priest. (page 137)

MCGILLIS, Frances Bertha: B-21, Frances Bertha McGillis, born 4 October 1906, baptized 5 October 1906, son of John McGillis and Adele Parent, Godfather: Alexandre Rivard, Godmother: Francoise Delorme, Alphonse Lemieux priest. (page 50)

MCGILLIS, Francois: Francois McGillis, age 7, died 17 March 1892, buried 18 March 1892, Witness: Prudent Lapointe, Pierre St.Germain priest. (page 138)

MCGILLIS, Georges: B-14, Georges McGillis, born 4 May 1908, baptized 6 May 1908, son of Gregoire McGillis and Helene Gosselin, Godfather: Georges Klyne, Godmother: Adele Gosselin, Alphonse Lemieux priest; married 21 October 193_, Elphee Laurte [?]. (page 54)

MCGILLIS, Gregoire Alfred and Helene GOSSELIN: M-4, Gregoire Alfred McGillis, adult son of Alexandre McGillis and Marie Jeannotte, married 31 October 1900, Helene Gosselin, minor daughter of Alexandre Gosselin and Marie Champagne, Witness: Jean Marie McGillis and Theophile McGillis, Pierre St.Germain o.m.i. (page 113)

MCGILLIS, Hyacinthe: B-21, Hyacinthe McGillis, born 11 September 1909, baptized 12 September 1909, son of Tobie McGillis and Marie Whiteford, Godfather: Napoleon Whiteford, Godmother: Rose Langan, Alphonse Lemieux priest; married 27 October 1931 Virginie Gaudry. (page 59)

MCGILLIS, Jean Baptiste: B-3, Jean Baptiste McGillis, born 10 May 1889, baptized 11 May 1889, son of Alexandre McGillis and Marie Jeannotte, Godfather: Modeste McGillis, Godmother: Marie Therese McGillis, Pierre St.Germain o.mi. (page 16)

MCGILLIS, Jean Joseph: B-5, Jean Joseph McGillis, born 21 March 1901, baptized 24 March 1901, son of Jean Marie McGillis and Eloiza Simpson, Godfather: Alex McGillis Sr., Godmother: Isabelle Fagnan, Pierre St.Germain o.m.i. (page 38)

MCGILLIS, Jean Marie: B-3, Jean Marie McGillis, born 6 February 1895, baptized 8 February 1895, son of Theophile McGillis and Josette Gosselin, Godfather: Jean Marie McGillis, Godmother: Isabelle Fagnan, A. Leuret priest; married, 11 February 1918, Marie Sophie Caplette. (page 26)

MCGILLIS, Joseph: Joseph McGillis, age 7 months, died 25 April 1900, buried 25 April 1900, Witness: Jean Marie McGillis, Emmanuel Garon priest. (page 138)

MCGILLIS, Joseph: B-15, Joseph McGillis. (page 48)

MCGILLIS, Joseph: B-4, Joseph McGillis, baptized 27 May 1890, son of Alexandre McGillis and Marie Jeannotte, Godfather: Isidore Ouellette, Godmother: Marie Botineau, Pierre St.Germain o.m.i. (page 18)

MCGILLIS, Joseph Alfred: B-6, Joseph Alfred McGillis, born 17 June 1892, baptized 18 June 1892, son of

St.Ignace Parish of Willow Bunch, Saskatchewan
1882-1910, Baptisms, Marriages and Burials

Theophile McGillis and Josette Gosselin, Godfather: Alexandre McGillis, Godmother: Marie Jeannotte, Pierre St.Germain o.m.i. (page 21)

MCGILLIS, Joseph Angus: B-12, Joseph Angus McGillis, born 15 June 1906, baptized 17 June 1906, son of Jean Marie McGillis and Marie Simpson, Godfather: Angus Alex. McGillis, Godmother: Sarah Simpson, Alphonse Lemieux priest. (page 50)

MCGILLIS, Joseph Edgard: B-9, Joseph Edgard McGillis, born 12 March 1908, baptized 15 March 1908, son of Theophile McGillis and Josette Gosselin, Godfather: Alexandre Gosselin, Godmother: Emelie Briere, Alphonse Lemieux priest. (page 54)

MCGILLIS, Joseph Magloire: B-3, Joseph Magloire McGillis, born 9 January 1903, baptized 18 January 1903, son of Tobie Pierre McGillis and Marie Whiteford, Godfather: Jean Marie McGillis, Godmother: Genevieve Leveillie, C. J. Passaplan priest. (page 42)

MCGILLIS, Joseph Martial: B-17, Joseph Martial McGillis, born 22 September 1899, baptized 10 October 1899, son of Jean Marie McGillis and Adele Dubreuil, Godfather: Alexandre McGillis, Godmother: Marie Jeannotte, Emmanuel Garon priest. (page 34)

MCGILLIS, Joseph Patrice: B-10, Joseph Patrice McGillis, born 10 August 1899, baptized 6 September 1899, son of William McGillis and Marie Rose Ouellette, Godfather: Louis Briere, Godmother: Josette Berard, Emmanuel Garon priest. (page 33)

MCGILLIS, Joseph Wilfrid: B-12, Joseph Wilfrid McGillis, born 17 July 1905, baptized 18 July 1905, son of Jean Marie McGillis and Adele Dubruil, Godfather: Gregoire McGillis, Godmother: Helene Gosselin, Alphonse Lemieux priest. (page 48)

MCGILLIS, Josephine: B-8, Josepine McGillis, born 20 May 1897, baptized 25 July 1897, Theophile McGillis and Josette Gosselin, Godfather: Alexandre McGillis Jr., Godmother: Adele Dubreuil, Pierre St.Germain o.m.i. (page 30)

MCGILLIS, Julien: B-6, Julien McGillis, born 13 March 1895, baptized 17 March 1895, son of William McGillis and Marie Rose Ouellette, Godfather: Narcisse Lacerte, Godmother: Seraphine Ouellete, A. Leuret priest. (page 26)

MCGILLIS, Laurent: B-17, Laurent McGillis, born 4 August 1903, baptized 17 August 1903, son of Louis McGillis and Marguerite Thomas, Godfather: Noel Baudry, Godmother: Marie Baudry, C. J. Passaplan priest. (page 43)

MCGILLIS, Louis Alexandre: B-9, Louis Alexandre McGillis, born 5 March 1903, baptized 7 March 1903, son of Theophile McGillis and Josette Gosselin, Godfather: Louis Briere, Godmother: Josette Briere, C. J. Passaplan priest; married 18 January 1827 Victoria Chartrand. (page 42)

MCGILLIS, Louis Desire: B-16, Louis Desire McGillis, born 9 July 1902, baptized 20 July 1902, son of Jean Marie McGillis and Marie Simpson, Godfather: Louis Napoleon McGillis, Godmother: Philomene Paul, C. J. Passaplan priest. (page 41)

MAGILLIS, Louis Riel and Marguerite THOMAS: M-2, Louis Riel McGillis, adult son of Modeste McGillis and Isabelle Poitras, married 21 May 1900, Marguerite Thomas, minor daughter of Bernard Thomas and Eloiza St.Denis, Witness: Guillaume Klyne and Rev. Pierre St.Germain o.m.i., Emmanuel Garon priest. (page 113)

MCGILLIS, M.: M. McGillis, age 34, buried 10 July 1910, Alphonse Lemieux priest. (page 140)

St.Ignace Parish of Willow Bunch, Saskatchewan
1882-1910, Baptisms, Marriages and Burials

MCGILLIS, Marguerite and Jean Marie WHITEFORD: M-2, Jean Marie Whiteford, adult son of Jean Marie Whiteford and _ Fagnan, married 29 December 1903, Marguerite McGillis, adult daughter of Modeste Modeste and Isabelle Poitras, Witness: Andre Gaudry and Joseph Botineau, C. J. Passaplan priest. (page 114)

MCGILLIS, Marie and Noel BAUDRY: M-2, Noel Baudry, son of Baptiste Baudry and Nancy Leveille, married 27 April 1892, Marie McGillis, daughter of Angus McGillis and Isabelle Fagnan, Witness: Napoleon Fagnan and Alexandre Fagnan, Pierre St.Germain o.m.i. (page 112)

MCGILLIS, Marie Agathe: B-7, Marie Agathe McGillis, born 29 May 1891, baptized 1 June 1891, daughter of Theophile McGillis and Josette Gosselin, Godfather: Jean Baptiste Caplette, Godmother: Francoise Delorme, Pierre St.Germain o.m.i.; married 25 July 1911, Zacharie Chartrand. (page 19)

MCGILLIS, Marie Beatrice: B-13, Marie Beatrice McGillis, born 4 September 1907, baptized 10 September 1907, daughter of Tobie McGillis and Marie Whiteford, Godfather: Napoleon McGillis, Godmother: Widow Angus McGillis, A. Lemieux priest. (page 52)

MCGILLIS, Marie Bibiane: B-1, Marie Bibiane McGillis, born 28 December 1904, baptized 8 January 1905, daughter of Jean Marie McGillis and Maria Simpson, Godfather: Alphonse Langer, Godmother: Philomene Baudry, C. J. Passaplan priest. (page 47)

MCGILLIS, Marie Emelie: B-13, Marie Emelie McGillis, born 24 October 1901, baptized 28 October 1901, daughter of Louis McGillis and Marguerite Thomas, Godfather: Louis Dumont, Godmother: Philomene Roussain, Pierre St.Germain o.m.i. (page 39)

MCGILLIS, Marie Emerence: B-17, Marie Emerence McGillis, born 17 September 1905, baptized 15 October 1905, daughter of Gregoire McGillis and Helene Gosselin, Godfather: Joseph McGillis, Godmother: Emerence Gosselin, Alphonse Lemieux priest. (page 48)

MCGILLIS, Marie Florestine: B-1, Marie Florestine McGillis, born 19 March 1888, baptized 29 March 1888, daughter of Modest McGillis and Isabelle Poitras, Godfather: Angus McGillis, Godmother: Isabelle McGillis, Pierre St.Germain o.m.i. (page 15)

MCGILLIS, Marie Joseph Georges: B-1, Marie Joseph Georges McGillis, born 12 January 1900, baptized 14 January 1900, son of Theophile McGillis and Josette Gosselin, Godfather: Emmanuel Garon priest, Godmother: Philomene Gosselin, Emmanuel Garon priest; married 17 February 1925, Clara Vermette. (page 35)

MCGILLIS, Marie Julie: B-5, Marie Julie McGillis, born 14 February 1908, baptized 15 February 1906, daughter of Jean Marie McGillis and Adele Dubrueil, Godfather: Francois Botineau, Godmother: Isabelle [?], Alphonse Lemieux priest. (page 53)

MCGILLIS, Marie Marceline: B-13, Marie Marceline McGillis, born 2 June 1902, baptized 3 June 1902, daughter of Jean Marie McGillis and Adele Parent [Dubray], Godfather: Joseph McGillis, Godmother: Josette Berard, C. J. Passaplan priest. (page 40)

MCGILLIS, Marie Mathilda: B-6, Marie Mathilda McGillis, born 17 March 1904, baptized 5 April 1904, daughter of Jean Marie McGillis and Adele Dubreuil, Godfather: Theophile McGillis, Godmother: Josette Gosselin, C. J. Passaplan priest. (page 45)

MCGILLIS, Marie Mathilde: B-2, Marie Mathilde McGillis, born 4 February 1905, baptized 12 February 1905, daughter of Theophile McGillis and Josette Gosselin, Godfather: Antoine Gosselin, Godmother: Helene Piche, C. J. Passaplan priest. (page 47)

MCGILLIS, Marie Philomene: B-12, Marie Philomene McGillis (twin), born 8 May 1902, baptized 8 May 1902, daughter of William John McGillis and Marie Rose Ouellette, Godfather: Alexandre Briere, Godmother: Marie Briere, Pierre St.Germain, o.m.i.; married Malta, 19 December 19__ James [...]. (page 40)

MCGILLIS, Marie Rose: Marie Rose McGillis, age _, died 6 November 1890, buried 8 November 1890, Witness: Joseph Lapointe, Pierre St.Germain priest. (page 137)

MCGILLIS, Marie Virginie: B-4, Marie Virginie McGillis, born 30 January 1899, baptized 15 February 1899, daughter of Theophile McGillis and Josette Gosselin, Godfather: Gregoire McGillis, Godmother: Marie Gosselin, Emmanuel Garon priest. (page 33)

MCGILLIS, Marie Virginie: Marie Virginie McGillis, age 3 weeks, died 24 February 1899, buried 20 February 1899, Witness: Gregoire McGillis, Emmanuel Garon priest. (page 138)

MCGILLIS, Mathilda and Alphonse LANGER: M-1, Alphonse Langer, adult son of David Langer and Marie Page, married 8 April 1901, Mathilda McGillis, adult daughter of Modeste McGillis and Isabelle Poitras, Witness: Pierre Briere and Francois Lafournaise, Pierre St.Germain o.m.i. (page 113)

MCGILLIS, Modeste: Modeste McGillis, died 11 October 1902, buried 12 October 1902, C. J. Passaplan. (page 139)

MCGILLIS, Pierre: Pierre McGillis, age 10, died 22 March 1892, buried 23 March 1892, Witness: Louis Dumais, Pierre St.Germain priest. (page 138)

MCGILLIS, Rose Anna: B-14, Rose Anna McGillis, born 28 October 1901, baptized 28 October 1901, daughter of Theophile McGillis and Josette Gosselin, Godfather: Delphis Short, Godmother: Rosalie Gosselin, Pierre St.Germain; married 16 June 1925, Moise St.Germain. (page 39)

MCGILLIS, Rose Athalie: B-14, Rose Athalie McGillis, born 9 May 1886, baptized 11 May 1886, daughter of Modeste McGillis and Isabelle Poitras, Godfather: Jerome Champagne, Godmother: Julie McGillis, Pierre St.Germain o.m.i. (page 11)

MCGILLIS, Rose Athalie and Joseph RAINVILLE: M-2, Joseph Rainville, son of Napoleon and Suzanne Poitras, married 11 May 1908, Rose Athalie McGillis, widow of Pierre Dumont, daughter of Modeste and Isabelle Poitras, Witness: Jean Baptiste Caplette and Jean Marie McGillis, Alphonse Lemieux priest. (page 115)

MCGILLIS, Therese and Francois BOTINEAU: M-1, Francois Botineau, married 7 January 1891, Therese McGillis, Witness: Joseph Short and Francois Lafournaise, Pierre St.Germain o.m.i. (page 112)

MCGILLIS, Theophile: B-17, Theophile McGillis, born 29 October 1893, baptized 25 December 1893, son of Theophile McGillis and Josette Gosselin, Godfather: Antoine Gosselin, Godmother: Therese McGillis, A. Leuret priest. (page 23)

MCGILLIS, Theophile and Josette GOSSELIN: M-1, Theophile McGillis, married 29 April 1890, Josette Gosselin, Witness: Antoine Gosselin and Alexandre McGillis, Pierre St.Germain o.m.i. (page 111)

MCGILLIS, Tobie and Marie WHITEFORD: M-5, Tobie McGillis, adult son of Angus McGillis and Isabelle

St.Ignace Parish of Willow Bunch, Saskatchewan
1882-1910, Baptisms, Marriages and Burials

Fagnan, married 28 October 1901, Marie Whiteford, minor daughter of Napoleon Whiteford and Marie Rose Langan, Witness: Zacharie Chartrand and Antoine Caplette, Pierre St.Germain o.m.i. (page 114)

MCGILLIS, Virginie: B-10, Virginie McGillis, born 4 June 1906, baptized 5 June 1906, daughter of Theophile McGillis and Josette Gosselin, Godfather: Joseph McGillis, Godmother: Marie Agathe McGillis, M. Mesnage vic. (page 49)

MCGILLIS, William John and Marie Rose OUELLETTE: M-2, John William McGillis, son of John McGillis and Marie Breland, married 4 February 1884, Marie Rose Ouellette, daughter of Francois Ouellette and Josette Botineau, Witness: Isidore Ouellette and Jean Louis Legare, Pierre St.Germain o.m.i. (page 110)

MITCHEL, Marie Rose and Georges CONNOR: M-1, Georges Connor, married 22 January 1884, Marie Rose Mitchel, Witness: Maxime Carrufel and Napoleon Myette, Pierre St.Germain o.m.i. (page 110)

MONDOR, Philippe and Marie Louise GRANGER: M-5, Philippe Mondor, son of Elie Mondor and Erminie Barrette, married 26 October 1909, Marie Louise Granger, daughter of Jean Louis Granger and Louise Legare, Witness: Conrad Legare and Romuald Granger, Alphonse Lemieux priest. (page 116)

MONZINI, Virginie: Virginie Mozini, age _, died 9 August 1891, buried 14 August 1891, Witness: Joseph Houle, Pierre St.Germain priest. (page 137)

MORIN, Antoine: B-7, Antoine Morin, born 27 September 1890, baptized 29 September 1890, son of Joseph Morin and Elisa Desjarlais, Godfather: Antoine Gosselin, Godmother: Helene Piche, Pierre St.Germain o.m.i. (page 18)

MORIN, Francois: B-11, Francois Morin, born 20 June 1885, baptized 21 June 1885, son of Joseph Morin and Elisa Desjarlais, Godfather: Francois Boxeur, Godmother: Josette Langer, Pierre St.Germain o.m.i. (page 8)

MORIN, Jean: Jean Morin, age 4, died 28 March 1894, buried 29 March 1894, Witness: Joseph Morin, A. Lerch, priest. (page 138)

MORIN, Jean Alfred: B-4, Jean Alfred Morin, born 21 May 1892, baptized 21 May 1892, son of Joseph Morin and Elisa Desjarlais, Godfather: Theophile McGillis, Godmother: Josette Gosselin, Pierre St.Germain o.m.i. (page 21)

MORIN, Jean Baptiste: B-2, Jean Baptiste Morin, born 26 March 1887, baptized 28 March 1887, son of Joseph Morin and Elisa Desjarlais, Godfather: Leonide Donais, Godmother: Angelique Morin, Pierre St.Germain o.m.i. (page 13)

MORIN, Jean Baptiste: B-15, Jean Baptiste Morin, born 26 June 1906, born 20 July 1906, son of Francois Morin and Justine Martin, Godfather: Joseph Morin, Godmother: Elisa Desjarlais, Alphonse Lemieux priest. (page 50)

MORIN, Jean Marie: B-13, Jean Marie Morin, born 29 June 1896, baptized 31 June 1896, son of Joseph Morin and Elisa Desjarlais, Godfather: Jean Marie Whiteford, Godmother: Isabelle Fagnan, Pierre St.Germain o.m.i. (page 29)

MORIN, Joseph: B-30, Joseph Morin, born 5 May 1883, baptized 18 September 1883, son of Joseph Morin and Helene Pelletier, Godfather: Andre Gaudry, Godmother: Marie Beauchamp, Pierre St.Germain o.m.i. (page 5)

MORIN, Joseph: Joseph Morin, age 5, died 6 March 1887, buried 7 March 1887, Witness: Jean Baptiste Cappelesse, Pierre St.Germain priest. (page 137)

MORIN, Justine: B-1, Justine Morin, born 7 October 1882, baptized 22 October 1882, daughter of Charles Morin and Marie Dauphinas, Godfather: Joseph Desmarais, Godmother: Rosalie St.Denis, Pierre St.Germain o.m.i. (page 1)

MORIN, Louis: B-19, Louis Morin, born 20 December 1893, baptized 25 December 1893, son of Joseph Morin and Elisa Desjarlais, Godfather: Louis R. McGillis, Godmother: Genevieve Whiteford, A. Leuret priest; married, 29 January 1918, Genevieve Gosselin. (page 24)

MORIN, Maria: B-26, Maria Morin, born 9 October 1908, baptized 13 October 1908, daughter of Francois Morin and Justine Martin, Godfather: Amable Gaudry, Godmother: Rosalie Morin, Alphonse Lemieux priest. (page 55)

MORIN, Marie Jeanne: B-2, Marie Jeanne Morin, born 7 January 1883, baptized 15 January 1883, daughter of Pierre Morin and Marguerite Hainault, Godfather: Moise Ouellette, Godmother: Veronique Dauphinais, Pierre St.Germain o.m.i. (page 2)

MORIN, Marie Julie: Marie Julie Morin, age 2-1/2, buried 25 July 1885, Witness: Francois Lafournaise, Pierre St.Germain priest. (page 137)

NOEL, Cecile: Cecile Noel, wife of Joseph Desnomme, age _, died 27 March 1890, buried 27 March 1890, Pierre St.Germain priest. (page 137)

NOLIN, Marie Louise: B-7, Marie Louise Nolin, born 2 May 1883, baptized 22 May 1885, daughter of Jean Nolin and Marie Tanner, Godfather: Jean Tanner, Godmother: Marie Lavallee, Pierre St.Germain o.m.i. (page 7)

OUELLETTE, Charles: B-8, Charles Valette, [Ouellette] born 8 January 1885, baptized 25 May 1885, son of Charles [Ouellette] and Francoise Pelletier, Godfather: Patrick Bradey, Godmother: Julie Pelletier, Pierre St.Germain o.m.i. (page 7)

OUELLETTE, Eleonore and Clement LACERTE: M-1, Clement Lacerte, son of Narcisse Lacerte and Julie Caplette, married 9 May 1898, Eleonore Ouellette, daughter of Isidore Ouellette and Marie Botineau, Witness: Isidore Ouellette and Narcisse Lacerte, Pierre St.Germain o.m.i. (page 113)

OUELLETTE, Eleonore: Eleonore Ouellette, wife of Clement Lacerte, age 37, died 21 March 1905, buried 22 March 1905, C. J. Passaplan priest. (page 139)

OUELLETTE, Elisabeth and Prudent LAPOINTE: M-3, Prudent Lapointe, son of Louis LaPointe and Adele Dugas, married 7 July 1886, Elisabeth Ouellette, daughter of Francois Ouellette and Josette Botineau, Witness: Isidore Ouellette and Joseph Lapointe, Pierre St.Germain o.m.i. (page 111)

OUELLETTE, Elisabeth LAPOINTE: Elisabeth Lapointe, wife of Prudent Lapointe, died 18 July 1910, buried 20 July 1910, Alphonse Lemieux priest. (page 140)

OUELLETTE, Eloisa and Joseph LAPOINTE: M-1, Joseph Lapointe, son of Louis Lapointe and Adele Dugas, married 16 July 1885, Eloisa Ouellette, daughter of Isidore Ouellette and Marie Botineau, Witness: _, Pierre St.Germain o.m.i. (page 111)

OUELLETTE, Georges: B-13, Georges Ouellette, born 15 September 1893, baptized 1 October 1893, son of Joseph Ouellette and Emerise Lafournaise, Godfather: Georges Klyne, Godmother: Louise Anne Klyne, Pierre St.Germain o.m.i. (page 23)

OUELLETTE, Isidore: Isidore Ouellette, age 76, died 15 May 1905, buried 17 May 1905, C. J. Passaplan priest.

(page 139)

OUELLETTE, Joseph: B-1, Joseph Ouellette, born 19 March 1887, baptized 19 March 1887, son of Joseph Ouellette and Emerise Lafournaise, Godfather: Isidore Ouellette, Godmother: Madeleine Poitras, Pierre St.Germain o.m.i. (page 13)

OUELLETTE, Joseph: Joseph Ouellette, son of Joseph Ouellette, age 21, died 3 October 1907, buried 11 October 1907, Alphonse Lemieux priest. (page 139)

OUELLETTE, Joseph and Emerise LAFOURNAISE: M-2, Joseph Ouellette, son of Isidore Ouellette and Marie Botineau, married 18 May 1886, Emerise Lafournaise, daughter of Joseph Lafournaise and Madeleine Poitras, Witness: Francois Lafournaise and Prudent Lapointe, Pierre St.Germain. (page 111)

OUELLETTE, Marie and Charles CHAMPAGNE: M-1, Charles Champagne married 6 January 1883 Marie Ouellette, Witness: Joseph Lapointe and Joseph Short, Pierre St.Germain o.m.i. (page 110)

OUELLETTE, Marie Rose and William John MCGILLIS: M-2, John William McGillis, son of John McGillis and Marie Breland, married 4 February 1884, Marie Rose Ouellette, daughter of Francois Ouellette and Josette Botineau, Witness: Isidore Ouellette and Jean Louis Legare, Pierre St.Germain o.m.i. (page 110)

OUELLETTE, Marie Adeline: B-4, Marie Adeline Ouellette, born 11 November 1882, baptized 12 November 1882, daughter of Ambroise Ouellette and Josephine Brien, Godfather: Isidore Ouellette, Godmother: Marie Botineau, Pierre St.Germain o.m.i. (page 1)

OUELLETTE, Marie Mathilde: B-12, Marie Mathilde Ouellette, born 27 June 1891, baptized 29 June 1891, daughter of Joseph Ouellette and Emerise Lafournaise, Godfather: William Klyne, Godmother: Marie Botineau, Pierre St.Germain o.m.i. (page 20)

OUELLETTE, Moise and Melanie PELLETIER: M-4, Moise Ouellette, married 14 April 1884, Melanie Pelletier, Witness: Elzear Botineau and Pierre Pelletier, Pierre St.Germain o.m.i. (page 110)

OUELLETTE, Seraphine and Narcisse LACERTE: M-1, Narcisse Lacerte, son of Narcisse Lacerte and Julie Caplette, married 8 January 1888, Seraphine Ouellette, daughter of Francois Ouellette and Josette Botineau, Witness: Isidore Ouellette and Joseph Short, Pierre St.Germain o.m.i. (page 111)

PAGE, Isidore: B-16, Isidore Page, born 17 June 1882, baptized 16 March 1883, son of Rene Page and Isabelle Desmarias, Godfather: William Cardinal, Godmother: Octavie Cardinal, Pierre St.Germain o.m.i. (page 3)

PAQUETTE, Marie Melida: Marie Melida Paquette, age 2 weeks, died 2 October 1898, buried 3 October 1898, Witness: Joseph Paquette, Emmanuel Garon priest. (page 138)

PAQUIN, Adelaird and Josephine HAMELIN: M-5, Adelard Paquin, son of Louis Paquin and Helene Gaudry, married 17 November 1908, Josephine Hamelin, daughter of Bernard Hamelin and Marie Briere, Witness: Louis Paquin and Pierre Briere, Alphonse Lemieux priest. (page 116)

PAQUIN, Rose Alma: B-20, Rose Alma Paquin, born 21 August 1909, baptized 22 August 1909, daughter of Adelard Paquin and Josephine Hamelin, Godfather: Alexandre Briere, Godmother: Therese Hamelin, Alphonse Lemieux priest; married 1) 10 November 1926 Joseph Georges Dufresne, married 2) Rover Simpson, Swan River, Manitoba. (page 58)

St.Ignace Parish of Willow Bunch, Saskatchewan
1882-1910, Baptisms, Marriages and Burials

PARENT, Jean Baptiste: B-15, Jean Baptiste Parent, born 2 December 1885, baptized 8 June 1886, son of Jean Parent and Marie Malaterre, Godfather: Andre Gaudry, Godmother: Marie Beauchamp, Pierre St.Germain o.m.i. (page 11)

PARENT, John: John Parent, age 43, buried 22 July 1913, Alphonse Lemieux priest. (page 141)

PARENT, Josephine:: Josephine Parent, died 25 May 1902, buried 15 September 1903, Witness: Joseph Parent, C. J. Passaplan. (page 139)

PARENT, Marguerite: Marguerite Parent, daughter of Johnny Parent, age 2, buried 14 April 1906, Alphonse Lemieux priest. (page 139)

PARENT, Marie Madeleine: B-16, Marie Madeleine Parent, born 11 November 1887, baptized 17 November 1887, daughter of Jean Parent and Marie Malaterre, Godfather: Narcisse Lacerte, Godmother: Catherine Cook, Pierre St.Germain o.m.i. (page 14)

PARENT, Marie Malvina: Marie Malvina Parent, age _, died 6 May 1888, buried 7 May 1888, Witness: Joseph Gosselin, Pierre St.Germain priest. (page 137)

PARKER, Norbert and Gelida BOULIANNE: M-3, Norbert Parker, son of Bernard Joseph Parker and Marie Anne Ward (Anglican), married 9 August 1909, Gelida Boulianne, daughter of Rieul Boulianne and Sarah Simard, Witness: Octave Rolli and Pascal Bonneau, Alphonse Lemieux priest. (page 116)

PAUL, Alfred: B-3, Joseph Alfred Paul, born 22 January 1902, baptized 27 January 1902, son of Joseph Paul and Louise Anne Klyne, Godfather: William Klyne, Godmother: Philomene Paul, Pierre St.Germain o.m.i. (page 39)

PAUL, Jean: B-16, Jean Paul, born 28 September 1900, baptized 29 September 1900, son of Joseph Paul and Louise Anne Klyne, Godfather: Francois Lafournaise, Godmother: Philomene Fagnan, Pierre St.Germain o.m.i. (page 36)

PAUL Jean: Jean Paul, age 1 day, died 29 September 1900, buried 30 September 1900, Witness: Joseph Paul, Pierre St.Germain priest. (page 138)

PAUL, Napoleon: B-33, Napoleon Paul, born 20 November 1908, baptized 6 December 1908, son of Joseph Paul and Louise Anne Klyne, Godfather: Georges Klyne, Godmother: Adele Gosselin, Alphonse Lemieux priest. (page 56)

PELLETIER, Charles: B-11, Charles Pelletier (illegitimate), born 20 March 1886, baptized 30 March 1886, son of parents unknown, Godfather: Moise Adam, Godmother: Marie Laplante, Pierre St.Germain o.m.i. (page 11)

PELLETIER, Jean Baptiste: B-19, Jean Baptiste Pelletier, born 19 March 1883, baptized 21 March 1883, son of Paul Pelletier and Louise Gonneville, Godfather: Jean Baptiste Beauchamp, Godmother: Melanie Pelletier, Pierre St.Germain o.m.i. (page 3)

PELLETIER, Jean Baptiste: Jean Baptiste Pelletier, age 4, buried 26 March 1891, Witness: Joseph Gosselin, Pierre St.Germain priest. (page 137)

PELLETIER, Josephine: Josephine Pelletier, wife of Antoine Amiotte, age _, died February 1881, buried 7 May 1887, Pierre St.Germain priest. (page 137)

PELLETIER, Melanie and Moise OUELLETTE: M-4, Moise Ouellette, married 14 April 1884, Melanie Pelletier,

Witness: Elzear Botineau and Pierre Pelletier, Pierre St.Germain o.m.i. (page 110)

PELLETIER, Louis: B-19, Louis Pelletier, born 15 December 1882, baptized 7 May 1883, son of Raphael Pelletier and Josette McGillis, Godfather: Ambroise Delorme, Godmother: Philomene Pelletier, Pierre St.Germain o.m.i. (page 4)

PELLETIER, Paul: Paul Pelletier, age 3, buried 22 June 1903, Witness: Israel Pelletier, C. J. Passaplan. (page 139)

PELLETIER, Philomene and Ambroise DELORME: M-4, Ambroise Delorme, married 28 April 1883, Philomene Pelletier, Witness: Joesph Lapointe and Pierre Pelletier, Pierre St.Germain o.m.i. (page 110)

PELLETIER, Pierre: Pierre Pelletier, age 55, died 11 November 1882, buried 25 November 1882, Witness: Jacques Pelletier, Pierre St.Germain priest. (page 137)

PELLETIER, William: B-5, William Pelletier, born 4 November 1885, baptized 26, March 1886, son of Emilien Pelletier and Caroline Laframboise, Godfather: William St.Denis, Godmother: Virginie Pelletier, Pierre St.Germain o.m.i. (page 10)

PERCHET, Louisa: B-1, Louisa Perchet, born 17 December 1885, baptized 11 January 1886, daughter of Louis Perchet and Alexandrine Riendeau, Godfather: Charles Riendeau, Godmother: Caroline Riendeau, Pierre St.Germain o.m.i. (page 10)

PERCHER, Louiza: Louiza Percher, age 3 months, buried 20 March 1886, Witness: O. Frarrell, Pierre St.Germain, priest. (page 137)

PERRAS, Eusebe Pierren and Virginie CHARTRAND: M-2, Eusebe Pierre Perras, son of Eusebe Perras and Ernestine Page, married 16 April 1907, Virginie Chartrand, daughter of Zacharie Chartrand and Victoire Breland, Witness: Gaspard Beaupre and Narcisse Lacerte, Alphonse Lemieux priest. (page 115)

PERRAS, Joseph: B-11, Joseph Perras, born 21 May 1909, baptized 6 June 1909, son of Pierre Perras and Virginie Chartrand, Godfather: Zacharie Chartrand, Godmother: Victoria Breland, Alphonse Lemieux priest; married Myrtle Jane Day. (page 57)

PERRAS, Marie Evelina: B-4, Marie Evelina Perras, born 21 January 1908, baptized 27 January 1908, daughter of Pierre Eusebe Perras and Virginie Chartrand, Godmother: Elise Chartrand, Alphonse Lemieux priest. (page 53)

PHILIPPON, Anne Marie: B-7, Anne Marie Philippon, born 18 April 1907, baptized 26 April 1907, daughter of Raoul Philippon and Denise Cuvier, Godfather: Octave Halle, Godmother: Angele Boulianne, M. Mesnage vic. (page 52)

PHILIPPON, Marcelle Marie Pauline: B-30, Marcelle Marie Pauline Philippon, born 10 October 1908, baptized 5 November 1908, daughter of Raoul Philippon and Denise Cuvier, Godfather: Emilie Philippon, Godmother: Pauline Cuvier, Alphonse Lemieux priest. (page 56)

PICARD, Genevieve: Genevieve Picard, age 70, buried 12 January 1888, Witness: Louis Dumais, Pierre St.Germain priest. (page 137)

PICHE, Aanonyme: 2 infants of Zacharie Piche, buried 13 July 1907, Alphonse Lemieux priest. (page 139)

PICHE, Anonyme: 2 infants of Zacharie Piche, buried 13 July 1907, Alphonse Lemieux priest. (page 139)

PICHE, Joseph Arsene: B-15, Joseph Arsene Piche, born 6 July 1909, baptized 11 July 1909, son of Zacharie Piche and Celina Briere, Godfather: Johnny Chartrand, Godmother: Veronique Chartrand, Alphonse Lemieux priest. (page 58)

PICHE, Joseph Marius Oscar: B-3, Joseph Marius Oscar Piche, born 21 July 1905, baptized 30 July 1905, son of Zacharie Piche and Celina Briere, Godfather: Jean Baptiste Dumais, Godmother: Vitaline Piche, Alphonse Lemieux priest. (page 48)

PICHE, Joseph Oscar: Joseph Oscar Piche, son of Zacharie Piche, age 7 months, buried 18 March 1906, M. Mesnage priest V. (page 139)

PICHE, Louis: B-28, Louis Piche, born 8 October 1886, baptized 10 October 1886, son of Louis Piche and Cecile Desmarais, Godfather: Gaspard Beaupre, Godmother: Florestine Piche, Pierre St.Germain o.m.i. (page 12)

PICHE, Louis: Louis Piche, age 59, died 15 January 1892, buried 16 January 1892, Witness: Joseph Gosselin, Pierre St.Germain priest. (page 137)

PICHE, Louis Arsene: B-15, Louis Arsene Piche, born 17 September 1896, baptized 7 November 1896, son of Zacharie Piche and Celina Briere, Godfather: Jean Chartrand, Godmother: Athalie Piche, Pierre St.Germain o.m.i. (page 29)

PICHE, Marie: B-2, Marie Piche, born 15 January 1899, baptized 15 February 1899, daughter of Zacharie Piche and Celina Briere, Godfather: Alexandre Briere, Godmother: Clemence Briere, Emmanuel Garon priest. (page 33)

PICHE, Marie Therese: Marie Therese Piche, age _, died 4 July 1883 [sic], buried 15 April 1884, Witness: Isidore Ouellette, Pierre St.Germain priest. (page 137)

PICHE, Marie Therese: B-23, Marie Therese Piche, born 11 December 1900, baptized 13 December 1900, daughter of Zacharie Piche and Celina Briere, Godfather: Antoine Gosselin Jr., Godmother: Helene Piche, Pierre St.Germain o.m.i. (page 37)

PICHE, Vitaline and Jean Baptiste DUMAIS: M-2, Jean Baptiste Dumais, son of Charles Dumais and Marie St.Arnaud, married 26 April 1893, Vitaline Piche, daughter of Louis Piche and Cecile Desmarais, Witness: Delphis Short and Louis Dumais, Pierre St.Germain o.m.i. (page 112)

PICHE, Zacharie and Celina BRIERE: M-1, Zacharie Piche, son of Louison and Cecile Desmarais, married 15 January 1895, Celina Briere, daughter of Jeremie Briere and Lisa Allary, Witness: Albert Legare and Johnny Chartrand, Albert Leuret priest. (page 113)

PIEUS, John: B-6, John Pieus (Indian), born 5 February 1886, baptized 28 March 1886, Parents Indian, Godfather: Joseph Tait, Godmother: Marguerite Desjarlais, Pierre St.Germain o.m.i. (page 10)

PLUMMER, Clara: B-3, Clara Plummer, born 12 April 1888, baptized 14 July 1888, daughter of Jean Plummer and Catherine Cook, Godfather: Pascal Bonneau Sr., Godmother: Seraphine Rainville, Pierre St.Germain o.m.i. (page 15)

PLUMMER, George: B-18, Georges Plummer, born 4 March 1886, baptized 4 March 1886, son of John Plummer and Catherine Cook, Godfather: Jean Baptiste Amyot, Godmother: Emerise Lafournaise, Pierre St.Germain o.m.i. (page 11)

POITRAS, Emelie: B-9, Emelie Poitras, born 25 October 1882, baptized 25 December 1882, daughter of Charles Poitras and Marie Breland, Godfather: Joseph Lapointe, Godmother: Victoire Breland, Pierre St.Germain o.m.i. (page 1)

POITRAS, Isabelle and Moise ADAM: M-4, Moise Adam, son of Baptiste Adam and Marie Bouille (Lac Pelletier), married 6 August 1909, Isabelle Poitras, daughter of Gabriel Poitras and Isabelle Malaterre, Witness: Alfred Lalonde and Albert Rainville, Alphonse Lemieux priest. (page 116)

POITRAS, Jules: B-5, Jules Poitras, born 31 March 1884, baptized 12 April 1884, son of Charles Poitras and Marie Breland, Godfather: Jean Louis Legare, Godmother: Eloiza Ouellette, Pierre St.Germain o.m.i. (page 6)

POITRAS, Madeleine: Madeleine Poitras, wife of Willie Klyne, age 69, buried 19 July 1909, Alphonse Lemieux priest. (page 140)

PRITCHARD, Victoire: B-9, Victoire Pritchard, born 29 May 1896, baptized 15 June 1896, daughter of Salomon Pritchard and Rosalie Trottier, Godfather: Jean Marie Trottier, Godmother: Ursule Trottier, Pierre St.Germain o.m.i. (page 28)

RAINVILLE, Alfred: B-13, Alfred Rainville, born 28 May 1903, baptized 31 May 1903, son of Napoleon Rainville and Philomene Klyne, Godfather: Joseph Paul, Godmother: Nathalie Trottier, C. J. Passaplan priest. (page 43)

RAINVILLE, Jean: B-29, Jean Rainville, born 1 May 1882, baptized 16 September 1883, son of Napoleon Rainville and Suzanne Poitras, Godfather: Guillaume Klyne, Godmother: Madeleine Poitras, Pierre St.Germain o.m.i. (page 5)

RAINVILLE, Joseph and Rose Athalie MCGILLIS: M-2, Joseph Rainville, son of Napoleon and Suzanne Poitras, married 11 May 1908, Rose Athalie McGillis, widow of Pierre Dumont, daughter of Modeste and Isabelle Poitras, Witness: Jean Baptiste Caplette and Jean Marie McGillis, Alphonse Lemieux priest. (page 115)

RAINVILLE, Jules: B-4, Jules Rainville, born 31 January 1906, baptized 1 February 1906, son of Napoleon Rainville and Philomene Klyne, Godfather: Francois Lafournaise, Godmother: Seraphine Houle, Alphonse Lemieux priest. (page 49)

RAINVILLE, Leander: Leandre Rainville, age 2, died 5 January 1883, buried 24 January 1883, Witness: Pierre Pelletier, Pierre St.Germain priest. (page 137)

RAINVILLE, Louise: Louise Rainville, age 1, buried 20 November 1887, Witness: Louis Dumais, Pierre St.Germain priest. (page 137)

RAINVILLE, Marie: B-31, Marie Rainville, born 31 October 1886, baptized 31 October 1886, daughter of Hilaire Rainville and Seraphine Houle, Godfather: Antoine Charbonneau, Godmother: Francoise Jerome, Pierre St.Germain o.m.i. (page 13)

RAINVILLE, Marie Philomene: B-28, Marie Philomene Rainville, born 29 October 1908, baptized 1 November 1908, daughter of Napoleon Rainville and Philomene Klyne, Godfather: Paul Rainville, Godmother: Louise Anne [Suzanne?] Poitras, Alphonse Lemieux priest; married 2 July 1931 Donat Joyal. (page 56)

RAINVILLE, Napoleon Carl and Philomene KLYNE: M-1, Napoleon Carl Rainville, adult son of Hilaire Rainville and Seraphine Houle, married 15 April 1902, Philomene Klyne, minor daughter of Guilluame Klyne and Madeleine Poitras, Witness: Raymond Gosslein and Georges Klyne, Pierre St.Germain o.m.i. (page 114)

St.Ignace Parish of Willow Bunch, Saskatchewan
1882-1910, Baptisms, Marriages and Burials

RICHARD, Marie: Marie Richard, age 12, buried 27 December 1910, A. Lemieux priest. (page 140)

RIVARD, Joseph and Josette LACERTE: M-1, Joseph Rivard, son of Alexandre Rivard and Francoise Delorme, married 4 January 1910, Josette Lacerte, daughter of Narcisse Lacerte and Seraphine Ouellette, Witness: Alexandre Rivard and Narcisse Lacerte, Alphonse Lemieux priest. (page 116)

RIVARD, Joseph Delphis: B-15, Joseph Delphis Rivard, born 14 February 1907, baptized 31 May 1908, Parents unknown, Godfather: Jean Riviere, Godmother: Sara Gosselin, married 26 December 1927, Victoria Dumais. (page 54)

RIVARD, Marie: B-16, Marie Rivard, born 24 May 1908, baptized 31 May 1908, Parents unknown, Godfather: Jean Riviere, Godmother: Sarah Gosselin, married 8 June 1926, Julien Beston. (page 54)

RIVIERE, Jean and Scholastique GOSSELIN: M-1, Jean Riviere, son of Jean Marie Riviere and Marie Leunard (of France), married 9 February 1909, Scholastique Gosselin, daughter of Antoine Gosselin and Helene Piche, Witness: Alexandre Rivard and Antoine Gosselin, Alphonse Lemieux priest. (page 116)

ROY, Angelique Lucie: B-22, Angelique Lucie Roy, born 28 October 1903, baptized 2 November 1903, daughter of Jean Baptiste Roy and Guillellmine Fagnan; Godfather: Alexandre Brien, Josette Brien, C. J. Passaplan priest. (page 43)

ROY, Caroline: B-11, Caroline Roy, born 30 March 1898, baptized 15 April 1898, daughter of Louis Roy and Marguerite Sauve, Godfather: Louis Joseph Haggeyt, Godmother: Guillelmine Fagnan, Emmanuel Garon priest. (page 32)

ROY, Emile: B-21, Emile Roy, born 5 December 1900, baptized 8 December 1900, son of Henri Roy and Helene Dumais, Godfather: Louis Roy, Godmother: Cecile St.Denis, Pierre St.Germain o.m.i. (page 37)

ROY, Emile: Emile Roy, age 6, died 6 December 1891, buried 7 December 1891, Witness: Baptiste Roy, Pierre St.Germain priest. (page 137)

ROY, Emile: Emile Roy, age 3 weeks, buried 27 December 1900, Witness: Henri Roy, Pierre St.Germain priest. (page 139)

ROY, Francois Louis: B-16, Francois Louis Roy, born 12 November 1895, baptized 8 December 1895, son of Louis Roy and Marguerite Sauve, A. Leurte priest. (page 27)

ROY, Henriette [Montagnaise dit CAYEN]: Henriette Roy, age 75, buried 20 November 1906, Alphonse Lemieux priest. (page 139)

ROY, Honore Pierre: B-17, Hornore Pierre Roy, born 12 November 1895, baptized 8 December 1895, son of Louis Roy and Marguerite Sauve, A. Leurte priest. (page 27)

ROY, Jean Baptiste and Lucie Guillemine FAGNAN: M-1, Jean Baptiste Roy, married 1 March 1892, Lucie Guillelmine Fagnan, daughter of Jean Baptiste Fagnan and Angelique Ward, Witness: Jean Baptiste Fagnan and Napoleon McGillis, Pierre St.Germain o.m.i. (page 112)

ROY, Joseph: Joseph Roy, age 1 month, died 5 May 1899, buried 6 May 1899, Witness: Louis Roy, Emmanuel Garon priest. (page 138)

St.Ignace Parish of Willow Bunch, Saskatchewan
1882-1910, Baptisms, Marriages and Burials

ROY, Joseph: Joseph Roy, died 25 December 1904, buried 14 May 1905, C. J. Passaplan. (page 139)

ROY, Joseph Francois: B-17, Joseph Francois Roy, born 9 November 1907, baptized 11 November 1907, son of Louis Roy and Marguerite Sauve, Godfather: Johnny Caplette, Godmother: Louise Leveille (dame Laplante), Alphonse Lemieux priest; married 9 April 1929 Marie Liza Short. (page 53)

ROY, Joseph Jimmy: B-7, Joseph Jimmy Roy, born 7 April 1899, baptized 7 April 1899, son of Louis Roy and Marguerite Sauve, Godfather: Zacharie Chartrand, Godmother: Vicoire Breland, Emmanuel Garon priest. (page 33)

ROY, Leon Emile: B-1, Leon Emile Roy, born 29 December 1892, baptized 3 January 1893, son of Baptiste Roy and Guillelmine Fagnan, Godfather: Louis Roy, Godmother: Marguerite Sauve, Pierre St.Germain o.m.i. (page 22)

ROY, Louis Joseph: B-13, Louis Joseph Roy, born 6 September 1889, baptized 22 September 1889, son of Louis Roy and Marguerite Lacerte, Godfather: Jean Baptiste Roy, Godmother: Marie St.Arnault, Pierre St.Germain o.m.i. (page 17)

ROY, Louis Joseph: B-7, Louis Joseph Roy, born 25 April 1905, baptized 14 May 1905, son of Baptiste Roy and Guillhelmine Fagnan, Godfather: Henri Roy, Godmother: Helene Dumais, C. J. Passaplan priest. (page 47)

ROY, Louis Joseph: Louis Joseph Roy, age 2, died 27 October 1891, buried 29 October 1891, Witness: Louis Dumais, Pierre St.Germain priest. (page 137)

ROY, Marguerite: B-16, Marguerite Roy, born 26 October 1893, baptized 25 December 1893, daughter of Louis Roy and Marguerite Sauve, Godfather: Louis Laplante, Godmother: Marie Roy, A. Leuret priest. (page 23)

ROY, Marguerite and Albert LAPOINTE: M-2, Albert Lapointe, son of Prudent Lapointe and Elisabeth Ouellette, married 20 April 1909, Marguerite Roy, daughter of Louis Roy and Marguerite Sauve, Witness: Louis Roy and Prudent Lapointe, Alphonse Lemieux priest. (page 116)

ROY, Marie Emilie: B-14, Marie Emilie Roy, 22 August 1885, baptized 13 September 1885, daughter of Louis Roy and Marguerite Sauve, Godfather: Louis Dumais, Godmother: Eloiza Caplette, Pierre St.Germain o.m.i. (page 8)

ROY, Marie Louise: B-8, Marie Louise Roy, born 17 April 1900, baptized 22 April 1900, Louis Roy and Marguerite Sauve, Godfather: Henri Roy, Godmother: Helene Dumais, Emmanuel Garon priest. (page 36)

ROY, Marie Phillipe Eugene: B-9, Marie Philippe Eugene Roy, born 30 April 1902, baptized 1 May 1902, son of Louis and Marguerite Sauve, Godfather: Joseph Plante, Godmother: Cecile St.Denis, Pierre St.Germain o.m.i.; married Battleford, 11 March 1926 Marie Virginie Laplante. (page 40)

ROY, Marie Rose: B-16, Marie Rose Roy, born 4 October 1899, baptized 8 October 1899, daughter of Jean Baptiste Roy and Wilhelmine Fagnan, Godfather: Joseph Gosselin, Godmother: Marie Rose Fagnan, Emmanuel Garon priest. (page 34)

ROY, Marie Rosina: B-11, Marie Rosina Roy, born 26 October 1898, baptized 4 September 1899, daughter of Henri Roy and Helene Dumais, Godfather: Louis Roy, Godmother: Marguerite Sauve, Emmanuel Garon priest. (page 34)

ROY, Marie Victoire: B-18, Marie Victoire Roy, born 1 November 1891, baptized 2 November 1891, daughter of Louis Roy and Marguerite Sauve, Godfather: Pierre St.Denis, Godmother: Marie Roy, Pierre St.Germain o.m.i. (page 20)

St.Ignace Parish of Willow Bunch, Saskatchewan
1882-1910, Baptisms, Marriages and Burials

ROY, Marie Victoria: Marie Victoria Roy, age 3, died 1 June 1894, buried 3 June 1894, Witness: Louis Dumais, A. Lerch priest. (page 138)

ROY, Marie Virginie: B-16, Marie Virginie Roy, born 6 September 1904, baptized 11 September 1904, daughter of Louis Roy and Marguerite Sauve, Godfather: Jean Baptiste Roy, Godmother: Virginie Laplante, C. J. Passaplan priest; married 29 July 1934 William Beston. (page 46)

ROY, William: B-6, William Roy, born 28 January 1902, baptized 24 February 1902, son of Jean Baptiste Roy and Guillelhmine Fagnan, Godfather: Jean Baptiste Fagnan, Godmother: Josette Roy, Pierre St.Germain o.m.i. (page 40)

SANDERSON, Georgina Theresa: B-21, Georgina Theresa Sanderson, born 20 October 1885, Moose Jaw, baptized 26 October 1885, daughter of George Sanderson and Mary Smith, Godfather: Thomas Murray, Godmother: Mary Moynihan, Pierre St.Germain o.m.i. (page 9)

SAUSE, Joseph Narcissse: B-3, Joseph Narcisse Sause, born 1884, baptized 30 March 1885, parents Indian, Godfather: Narcisse Lacerte, Pierre St.Germain o.m.i. (page 7)

SHIELDS, Cornelia Theresa: B-18, Cornelia Theresa Shields, born 20 July 1884, Medicine Hat, baptized 20 July 1885], daughter of Cornelius Shields and Theresa McHugh, Godfather: Christof Kevin, Godmother: Alice McHugh, Fay, priest. (page 8)

SHIELDS, Martin Cornelius: B-17, Martin Cornelius Shields, 25 September 1885, Medicine Hat, baptized 7 October 1885, son of Cornelius Shields and Theresa McHugh, Godfather: John McHugh, Godmother: Elisabeth Kevin, Emarried Segal o.m.i. (page 8)

SHORT, Caroline: B-5, Caroline Short, born 6 March 1896, baptized 18 March 1896, daughter of Dolphis Short and Rosalie Gosselin, Godfather: Zacharie Chartrand, Godmother: Marie Gosselin, A. Leuret priest. (page 28)

SHORT, Caroline: Caroline Short, daughter of Delphis Short, age 10, buried 27 June 1907, Alphonse Lemieux priest. (page 139)

SHORT, Delphis and Rosalie GOSSELIN: M-1, Delphis Short, son of Joseph Short and Marguerite Houle, married 24 April 1894, Rosalie Gosselin, daughter of Antoine Gosselin and Françoise Delorme, Witness: Joseph Lapointe and Jean Louis Legare, Pierre St.Germain o.m.i., Albert Leuret priest. (page 112)

SHORT, Emile: B-22, Emile Short, born 21 September 1902, baptized 3 October 1902, son of Delphis Short and Rosalie Gosselin, Godfather: Raymond Gosselin, Godmother: Victoire Chartrand, C. J. Passaplan priest, married, 2 June 1922 [?], Marie Lucie Dumais. (page 41)

SHORT, Joseph: B-2, Joseph Short, born 4 February 1895, baptized 5 February 1895, son of Dolphis Short and Rosalie Gosselin, Godfather: Johnny Gosselin, Godmother: Francoise Delorme, A. Leuret priest. (page 26)

SHORT, Joseph and Josette BOTINEAU: M-3, Joseph Short, married 30 May 1887, Josette Botineau, Witness: Louis Piche and Joseph Botineau, Pierre St.Germain o.m.i. (page 111)

SHORT, Joseph Louis : B-7, Joseph Louis Short, born 29 October 1898, baptized 1 November 1898, son of Delphis Short and Rosalie Gosselin, Godfather: Antoine Gosselin, Godmother: Helene Piche, Emmanuel Garon priest. (page 32)

SHORT, Leon: B-22, Leon Short, born 31 October 1906, baptized 9 November 1906, son of Delphis Short and Rosalie Gosselin, Godfather: Narcisse Lacerte, Godmother: Seraphine Ouellette, Alphonse Lemieux priest; married Regina 2 October 19__ Jeanne Beaupre. (page 51)

SHORT, Louis: Louis Short, buried 7 June 1900, age 1, Witness: Dolphis Short, Pierre St.Germain priest. (page 138)

SHORT, Louis Desire: B-9, Louis Desire Short, born 15 May 1905, baptized 18 May 1905, son of Delphis Short and Rosalie Gosselin, Godfather: Theophile McGillis, Godmother: Josette Gosselin, C. J. Passaplan priest. (page 47)

SHORT, Marguerite: B-20, Marguerite Short, born 28 November 1900, baptized 4 December 1900, daughter of Dolphis Short and Rosalie Gosselin, Godfather: Joseph Gosselin, Godmother: Marie Rose Fagnan, Pierre St.Germain o.m.i., married 16 June 1925, Joseph Marie Chartrand. (page 37)

SHORT, Marie Lisa: B-29, Marie Lisa Short, born 2 November 1908, baptized 5 November 1908, daughter of Delphis Short and Rosalie Gosselin, Godfather: Alexandre Gosselin, Godmother: Emelie Briere, Alphonse Lemieux priest; married 9 April 1929 Joseph Francois Roy. (page 56)

SHORT, Marie Rose: B-7, Marie Rose Short, born 8 May 1897, baptized 25 July 1897, daughter of Delphis Short and Rosalie Gosselin, Godfather: Jean Marie Whiteford, Godmother: Genevieve Whiteford, Pierre St.Germain o.m.i.; married 7 February 1922, St.Pierre Chartrand. (page 30)

SINCLAIR, Georges: B-11, Georges Sinclair, born January 1880, baptized 20 May 1885, son of William Sinclair and Marie Chartrand, Godfather: Francois Delorme, Godmother: Marie Roy, Pierre St.Germain o.m.i. (page 8)

SIOUX, Marie Anne Marguerite: B-8, Marie Anne Marguerite Sioux, born 14 April 1884, Godfather: Pierre St.Germain [priest], Godmother: Marguerite Patenaude, Pierre St.Germain o.m.i. (page 6)

ST.DENIS, Henri: B-14, Henri St.Denis, born 7 March 1891, born 20 September 1891, son of Pierre St.Denis and Josette Roy, Godfather: Louis Dumais, Godmother: Eleonore Ouellette, Pierre St.Germain o.m.i. (page 20)

ST.DENIS, Isidore: Isidore St.Denis, died 28 June 1902, buried 30 June 1902, Witness: St.Denis pere, C. J. Passaplan. (page 139)

ST.DENIS, Jean Baptiste: B-1, Jean Baptiste St.Denis, born 12 January 1889, baptized 13 January 1889, son of Pierre St.Denis and Josette Roy, Godfather: Joseph Laplante, Godmother: Eloiza Caplette, Pierre St.Germain o.m.i. (page 16)

ST.DENIS, Jean Baptiste: Jean Baptiste St.Denis, age 2, buried 11 April 1891, Witness: Paul Caplette, Pierre St.Germain priest. (page 137)

ST.DENIS, Joseph Emile: B-15, Joseph Emile St.Denis (illegitimate), born 15 February 1899, baptized 16 June 1899, son of Johnny St.Denis and Nancy Comtois, Godfather: Louis Haggeyt (son), Godmother: Marguerite Sauve, Emmanuel Garon priest. (page 34)

ST.DENIS, Patrice: B-11, Patrice St.Denis, born 5 July 1893, baptized 6 August 1893, son of Pierre St.Denis and Josette Roy, Godfather: Louis Roy, Godmother: Marie Roy, Pierre St.Germain o.m.i.; married, 12 January 1923, Josette Lacerte. (page 22)

ST.DENIS, Philomene and Joseph LAROCQUE: M-2, Joseph Larocque, son of Baptiste Larocque and Julie

Lemieux, married 14 October 1895, Philomene St.Denis, daughter of Pierre St.Denis and Adelaide Dauphinais, Witness: Isidore Ouellette and Antoine Caplette, Albert Leuret priest. (page 113)

ST.DENIS, Pierre: Pierre St.Denis, buried 17 December 1894, A. Lerch priest. (page 138)

ST.GERMAIN, Philomene: B-10, Philomene St.Germain, born 16 February 1883, baptized 18 February 1883, daughter of Charles St.Germain and Angelique Lafournaise, Godfather: Joseph Short, Godmother: Marguerite Houle, Pierre St.Germain o.m.i.

ST.GERMAIN, Philomene: Philomene St.Germain, age 1, died 23 February 1884, buried 25 February 1884, Witness: Joseph Short, Pierre St.Germain priest. (page 137)

SUREAU, Maurice: Maurice Sureau, without a spouse, age 35, buried 25 October 1909, Alphonse Lemieux priest. (page 140)

THOMAS, Adelaide and Joseph BOTINEAU: M-3, Joseph Botineau, son of Joseph Botineau and Louise Vallee, married 7 November 1895, Adelaide Thomas, daughter of Francois Thomas and Marie Adele _, Witness: Albert Legare and Albert Beauchamp, Albert Leuret priest. (page 113)

THOMAS, Bernard and Marie GOSSELIN: M-2, Bernard Thomas, son of Joseph Thomas and Marie Adele _, married 15 May 1906, Marie Gosselin, daughter of Antoine Gosselin and Francoise Delorme, Witness: Louis Dumont and Francois Lafournaise, M. Mesnage priest. (page 115)

THOMAS, Louis and Rosalie DUMONT: M-1, Louis Thomas, son of Bernard Thomas and Lisa St.Denis, married 4 May 1908, Rosalie Dumont, daughter of Louis Dumont and Philomene Roussin, Witness: Tobie McGillis and Pierre Lavallee, Alphonse Lemieux priest. (page 115)

THOMAS, Marguerite and Louis Riel MCGILLIS: B-2, Louis Riel McGillis, adult son of Modeste McGillis and Isabelle Poitras, married 21 May 1900, Marguerite Thomas, minor daughter of Bernard Thomas and Eloiza St.Denis, Witness: Guillaume Klyne and Rev. Pierre St.Germain o.m.i., Emmanuel Garon priest. (page 113)

THOMAS; Pierre: B-2, Pierre Thomas, born 28 January 1909, baptized 21 February 1909, son of Louis Thomas and Rosalie Dumont, Godfather: Louis Dumont, Godmother: Philomene Roussin, Alphonse Lemieux priest. (page 57)

TROTTIER, Athalie and Antoine CAPLETTE: M-1, Antoine Caplette, son of Antoine Caplette and Seraphine Houle, married 13 February 1893, Athalie Trottier, daughter of Jean Baptiste Trottier and Rose McGillis, Witness: Napoleon McGillis and Theophile McGillis, Pierre St.Germain o.m.i. (page 112)

TROTTIER, Marie Rose: B-17, Marie Rose Trottier, born 1885, baptized 8 March 1886, daughter of Alexandre Trottier and Catherine Laframboise, Godfather: Francois Tait, Godmother: Louise Boyer, Pierre St.Germain o.m.i. (page 11)

WALLDRON, Edith Kathleen: B-22, Edith Kathleen Walldron, born 28 April 1883, baptized 15 May 1883, daughter of W. J. Waldron and Rose Therese Doherty, Godfather: Pascal Bonneau, Godmother: Celina Bonneau, Pierre St.Germain o.m.i. (page 4)

WALLDRON, Wallace Edmond: B-1, Wallace Edmond Walldron, born 8 January 1885, baptized 19 March 1885, son of Thomas Walldron and Rose Doherty, Godfather: Edward McCarthy, Godmother: Julia McCarthy, Pierre St.Germain o.m.i. (page 7)

St.Ignace Parish of Willow Bunch, Saskatchewan
1882-1910, Baptisms, Marriages and Burials

WARD, Angelique: Angelique Ward, wife of Jean Baptiste Fagnant, age 60, died 19 January 1902, buried 21 January 1902, Pierre St.Germain priest. (page 139)

WHITEFORD, Jean Jacques: B-7, Jean Jacques Whiteford, born 24 March 1906, baptized 26 March 1906, son of Jean Marie Whiteford and Marguerite McGillis, Godfather: Alexandre McGillis, Godmother: Nathalie _, M. Mesnage vic. (page 49)

WHITEFORD, Jean Marie and Marguerite MCGILLIS: M-2, Jean Marie Whiteford, adult son of Jean Marie Whiteford and _ Fagnan, married 29 December 1903, Marguerite McGillis, adult daughter of Modeste Modeste and Isabelle Poitras, Witness: Andre Gaudry and Joseph Botineau, C. J. Passaplan priest. (page 114)

WHITEFORD, Jean Napoleon: B-14, Jean Napoleon Whiteford, born 14 June 1909, baptized 15 June 1909, son of Napoleon Whiteford and Marie Rose Langan, Godfather: Jean Marie Whiteford, Godmother: Genevieve Whiteford, Alphonse Lemieux priest; married Elizabeth Falcon, 18 September 1930 [?] Great Falls, Montana. (page 58)

WHITEFORD, Jimmy and Marie Celina LANGER: M-3, Jimmy Whiteford, son of Jimmy Whiteford and Sarah Gladu, married 14 October 1907, Marie Celina Langer, daughter of David Langer and Marie Page, Witness: David Langer and Jean Baptiste [Marie?] Whiteford, Alphonse Lemieux priest. (page 115)

WHITEFORD, Jimmy: Jimmy Whiteford, age 83, died 19 November 1908, buried 21 November 1908, Witness: Dr. Godin, Alphonse Lemieux priest. (page 139)

WHITEFORD, Joseph Marie: B-18, Joseph Marie Whiteford, born 23 November 1907, baptized 1 December 1907, son of Jean Marie Whiteford and Marguerite McGillis, Godfather: Norbert McGillis, Godmother: Isabelle Poitras, Alphonse Lemieux priest. (page 53)

WHITEFORD, Joseph Maxime: B-5, Joseph Maxime Whiteford, born 23 November 1903, baptized 15 April 1905, son of Napoleon Whiteford and Marie Rose Langan, Godfather: Jean Marie McGillis, Godmother: Maria Simpson, C. J. Passaplan priest. (page 47)

WHITEFORD, Louis Ovila: B-6, Louis Ovila Whiteford, born 31 March 1901, baptized 1 April 1901, son of Napoleon Whiteford and Marie Rose Langan, Godfather: Jean Marie Whiteford, Godmother: Genevieve Whiteford, Pierre St.Germain o.m.i. (page 38)

WHITEFORD, Louis Pierre: B-11, Louis Pierre Whiteford, born 19 September 1902, baptized 21 April 1903, son of Napoleon Whiteford and Marie Langan, Godfather: Ambroise Chartrand, Godmother: Francois Gaudry, C. J. Passaplan priest. (page 43)

WHITEFORD, Marie and Tobie MCGILLIS: M-5, Tobie McGillis, adult son of Angus McGillis and Isabelle Fagnan, married 28 October 1901, Marie Whiteford, minor daughter of Napoleon Whiteford and Marie Rose Langan, Witness: Zacharie Chartrand and Antoine Caplette, Pierre St.Germain o.m.i. (page 114)

WHITEFORD, Marie Delima: B-11, Marie Delima Whtieford (illegitimate), born 6 August 1895, baptized 16 June 1896, daughter of Eli (Heli) Whiteford and an Indian, Godfather: Patrice Trottier, Godmother: Marie Rose Whiteford, Pierre St.Germain o.m.i. (page 29)

WHITEFORD, Marie Flora: B-17, Marie Flora Whiteford, born 7 October 1904, baptized 9 October 1904, daughter of Jean Marie Whiteford and Marguerite McGillis, Godfather: Jimmy Whiteford, Godmother: Genevieve Whiteford, C. J. Passaplan priest. (page 46)

St.Ignace Parish of Willow Bunch, Saskatchewan
1882-1910, Baptisms, Marriages and Burials

WHITEFORD, Marie Pruscielle: B-3, Marie Pruceille Whiteford, born 7 March 1909, baptized 8 March 1909, daughter of Jean Marie Whiteford and Marguerite McGillis, Godfather: Zacharie Chartrand, Godmother: Victoire Breland, Alphonse Lemieux priest; married 20 January 1926 Georges Pritchard. (page 57)

WHITEFORD, Pierre: B-1, Pierre Whiteford, born 6 January 1909, baptized 8 January 1909, son of Jimmy Whiteford and Marie Celina Langer, Godfather: Xavier Langer, Godmother: Marie Page, Alphonse Lemieux priest. (page 57)

WIZI, Joseph: B-17, Joseph Wizi (Sioux), born 1900, baptized 20 August 1902, son of Amos Wizi and Ida Sdawin, Godfather: C. J. Passaplan priest, Godmother: Rosine Champagne, C. J. Passaplan priest. (page 41)

WIZI, Marie Josephine Amos: B-9, Marie Josephine Amos Wizi (Sioux), born December 1903, baptized 1 May 1904, daughter of Amos Wizi and Melley _, Godfather: Francois Lafournaise, Godmother: Genevieve Whiteford, C. J. Passaplan priest. (page 45)

www.ingramcontent.com/pod-product-compliance
Lightning Source LLC
Chambersburg PA
CBHW081415280526
45788CB00009B/3117